Teresa Fish

The **Girl Scout** Promise*

ON MY HONOR, I WILL TRY:

To serve God,

My country and mankind,

And to live by the Girl Scout Law.

ADULT

JUNIOR

SENIOR

CADETTE

BROWNIE

The Girl Scout Law*

I will do my best:

—to be honest

—to be fair

—to help where I am needed

—to be cheerful

—to be friendly and considerate

—to be a sister to every Girl Scout

—to respect authority

—to use resources wisely

—to protect and improve the world around me

—to show respect for myself and others through my
words and actions

*New wording adopted by the National Council of Girl Scouts of the U.S.A., October 1972.

Catalog No. 20-602 $1.50
ISBN 0-88441-314-4

Girl Scouts of the United States of America
830 Third Avenue, New York, N.Y. 10022

JUNIOR

GIRL SCOUT HANDBOOK

CONTENTS

THE PATH

The path of Scouting is a fun filled path. Every step along the way is filled with adventure.

You'll hike in the sun, in the snow, in the rain. You'll explore on foot, take a bus, or a train. Camp under a tree. Learn to fix a scratched knee.

Indoors, too, there's plenty to do. You'll cook and sew, tell stories you know. Put on a play, make figures of clay, make bracelets and rings—all kinds of things. You'll celebrate special Scout days in special Scout ways.

You travel along this path with your troop—other girls who are 9 or 10 or 11 years old—and a grownup leader who likes girls and likes to do the things Girl Scouts do.

The first thing you do is to learn about special Girl Scout ways to get ready to become a Junior Girl Scout. You will learn these during your first four troop meetings, maybe more.

You learn the Girl Scout Promise—and the Girl Scout Law.

You find out about the special sign Girl Scouts make and what it means.

You discover the secret handshake Girl Scouts use whenever they meet each other.

You learn the meaning of the Girl Scout motto—Be Prepared —and the slogan—Do a Good Turn Daily.

If you were in a Brownie troop and are already a Girl Scout, you become a Junior Girl Scout at a REDEDICATION ceremony. At this ceremony you make your Girl Scout Promise. You say you will try to live the Girl Scout Law. You wear your green uniform for the first time and your leader pins your Girl Scout pin on you.

If you have never been a Girl Scout before, you become a Junior Girl Scout at an INVESTITURE ceremony. At this ceremony you make your Girl Scout Promise. You say you will try to live the Girl Scout Law. You wear your green uni-

uniform for the first time and your leader pins your Girl Scout pin on you.

Along the path are all the hundreds of things Girl Scouts like to do, indoors and out. You and your troop decide which.

You can work on badges

 Earn the Sign of the Arrow

 And the Sign of the Star

Some of these you do with all the girls in your troop.

Others you do with a small group in the troop called a patrol.

Some you may even do with girls from other troops and with girls at a Girl Scout camp.

From time to time along the path, you meet older Girl Scouts —Cadettes and Seniors—and have a chance to help Brownie Scouts. You can recognize them by their uniforms.

On the path with you are millions of other girls. You cannot see them all from where you stand. But they are there. They are the Girl Scouts and Girl Guides in countries round the world. They all wear the pin of the World Association of Girl Guides and Girl Scouts. You will too.

As you travel along the path, you celebrate many special Girl Scout days...the birthday of Juliette Low, Founder of Girl Scouting in this country...Girl Scout Week...Thinking Day.

Just around the last bend in the path lies a bridge. When you are twelve, you cross the bridge and become a Cadette Girl Scout.

* * * * * * * * * * *

MEMBERSHIP REQUIREMENTS

1. Be 9, 10, or 11 years old or in the 4th, 5th, or 6th grade.

2. Attend at least four troop meetings.

3. Pay annual national membership dues.

4. Make the Girl Scout Promise and accept the Girl Scout Law.

* * * * * * * * * * *

TROOP MEETINGS

At troop meetings you and your troop do all kinds of Girl Scout things.

Some of the time you meet inside—in the troop room—and go outside for a while. Sometimes you meet outside and go some place—to a park or someone's backyard.

Girl Scout meetings open with a ceremony, a game, a song. Sometimes all the girls will say the Promise and Law. Another time one girl will read a poem to the whole troop. Your troop makes up its own ceremonies. Every meeting is different.

Then you do something new. At your first few meetings you get to know everyone in your troop, You learn the Promise and Law and all the special Girl Scout ways. You learn songs and games and you work on badges. When your troop has patrols, you will learn new things with your patrol.

There is business to attend to. At the first meeting of the year, your troop must decide how you will keep your meeting room neat. Where will you put your coat and school books and troop equipment? Who will clean up after each meeting?

You plan the next meeting so you will know what to bring and be ready to do your part. Sometimes the meeting you plan will be a party or a campfire meeting or a ride on a ferry. Sometimes you plan a camping trip.

At every meeting your troop has plans to talk about. Sometimes plans are made by patrols, sometimes by the troop.

As the meeting ends you have a closing ceremony. Your troop will plan that too.

Then, the girls whose turn it is to clean up make the troop room neat, and they help the troop leader with anything she has to carry.

This is what a troop meeting is like.

On the next page you'll find things to do at your first meetings and what you need to know to be a Girl Scout.

On your mark. Get set. Go!

THE GIRL SCOUT QUIET SIGN

Girl Scouts use the quiet sign at all their meetings—troop meetings, patrol meetings, camp meetings. The person in charge of the meeting raises her right hand high. When you see her hand, you stop talking and raise your hand. Soon everyone sees the sign and all is quiet.

✳ ✳ ✳ ✳ ✳ ✳ ✳ ✳

GET SET. GO!

This handbook is full of things to do. Here are ideas for things your troop can do right now.

SING!

* Sing to start or end your meeting. Try "Whene'er You Make a Promise" on page 192.
* Sing just for the fun of it. "Gypsy Song" on page 193 is a fun song from another country.

MAKE SOMETHING!

* Make a sewing box you can use at home or at troop meetings. Look at the one on page 221.
* Make a drawstring bag big enough to hold your *Girl Scout Handbook*, paper, a pencil, things you need for a troop meeting or a hike. Make the bag on page 225.

GO HIKING!

* Go some place you've never been before or return to a favorite spot. See chapter on "Going Places."
* Explore the streets of your town or follow a stream or climb a hill.
* Visit the zoo or the park or the open air market.
* Cook Somemores over a fire in someone's backyard. Fires are on pages 110-121 and Somemores on page 140.

DO A GOOD TURN!

* Leave some place better than you found it (page 299). Fix your troop meeting place so that it is even neater and cleaner.
* Give your leader a hand when she has things to carry.

PLAY A GAME!

* Run, Skip, Jump on page 157 will warm you up.
* Kim's Game on page 159 will show how sharp your eyes are.
* Make a contest out of something you have just learned to do. Learn to make a fire (pages 110-116) and then play the string burning game (page 160).

BE PREPARED!

* Make a troop first aid kit (pages 302-303). See that every item is labeled.
* Learn to tie a square knot (page 96) so you can tie your tie or fasten a package.
* Learn to set a table (pages 148-149) so you can help at home.

DISCOVER THE WAYS OF A GIRL SCOUT!

* Learn the ways of a Girl Scout (pages 21-25). Practice the sign and the handshake with the other girls.
* Find out how Girl Scouting started (pages 26-28). Talk about how you follow the Promise and the Law at home, at school, at troop meetings.

PROMISE & LAW

The Girl Scout Promise is a way Girl Scouts promise to act every day toward one another and other people.

The Girl Scout Promise

On my honor, I will try:

To serve God,

My country and mankind,

And to live by the Girl Scout Law.

It's not such an easy promise to keep! What do the words mean?

You are promising to try to do your very best:

- to serve God in the best way you know. This includes respecting the beliefs of others whose religion may be different than yours.

- to be a good citizen and to help others whenever you can.

- to try to remember and follow the Girl Scout Law every day in all you do.

Laws are made to help people get along together. The Girl Scout Law outlines a way for Scouts to act towards other people and their world.

The Girl Scout Law

I will do my best:

to be honest

to be fair

to help where I am needed

to be cheerful

to be friendly and considerate

to be a sister to every Girl Scout

to respect authority

to use resources wisely

to protect and improve the world around me

to show respect for myself and others through my words and actions

Look at the Girl Scout Law and see if you know what each part means. Try to think of a time when you have followed each part of the Law by the way you have acted.

A CLOSER LOOK
at the
GIRL SCOUT LAW

Take a closer look at the meaning of the key words in each part of the Girl Scout Law. This will help you understand the Law better.

—to be **honest**

> Being **honest** is being truthful about what you say and do.

–to be **fair**

> Being **fair** means treating everyone equally.

—to **help** where I am **needed**

> **Helping** when **needed** means you will do what you can when it can be useful to someone else.

–to be **cheerful**

> Being **cheerful** means being nice to everyone even when you're not really happy.

—to be **friendly** and **considerate**

> Treating others the way you like being treated is being **friendly** and **considerate.**

–to be a **sister** to every Girl Scout

> Being a **sister** to all Scouts means that you're a friend to every Girl Scout you meet.

—to **respect authority**

> **Respecting authority** is following the direc-
> tions of the person who is in charge.

—to **use resources wisely**

> **Resources** are the things you own, the things
> you can do, and the things you use in the
> natural world; **using** them **wisely** means you
> will use them carefully and the best way you
> know.

—to **protect** and **improve** the **world** around me

> When you are a friend to animals, plants, and
> the earth, as well as people, and try whenever
> you can to make the world a better place, you
> are **protecting** and **improving** the **world.**

—to show **respect for myself and others** through my words
and actions

> When the things you say and do show that you
> are proud of yourself and that you care about
> other people, you are showing **respect for
> yourself and others.**

Just like the Girl Scout Promise, the Girl Scout Law is not
easy to put into practice every day. Talk about the Girl Scout
Law with members of your troop or patrol. See if you can do
something to put each of the parts of the Law to work for you.
Then ask yourself if following the Law helped you get along
with someone better or made someone else a bit happier.

WAYS OF A GIRL SCOUT

Now you know the Girl Scout Promise and Law.

What else is special about Girl Scouts?

BE PREPARED is the Girl Scout motto. Girl Scouts learn to do things so they are ready for bigger adventures, so they are ready to help.

DO A GOOD TURN DAILY is the Girl Scout slogan. Good turns are kind things you do without being asked. They make other people happy. You do not receive a reward, but you feel good inside.

A service project is a special kind of a good turn that Girl Scouts plan to do. It is bigger. It takes more planning and more time. You may need to learn something new to help on a service project. If your troop is going to plant trees at your school, you have to learn how first.

You can share your fun with others. Your troop or your patrol can serenade a girl who can't go out. You can invite a new girl to visit your troop and join your games at school.

You can use your skills to do a service project. When you learn how to make toys, you can make them for a lonely child.

You can give your time to do a service project. Your troop may be asked to help at your council office, sorting clothes. You give an afternoon and make a big job possible.

11

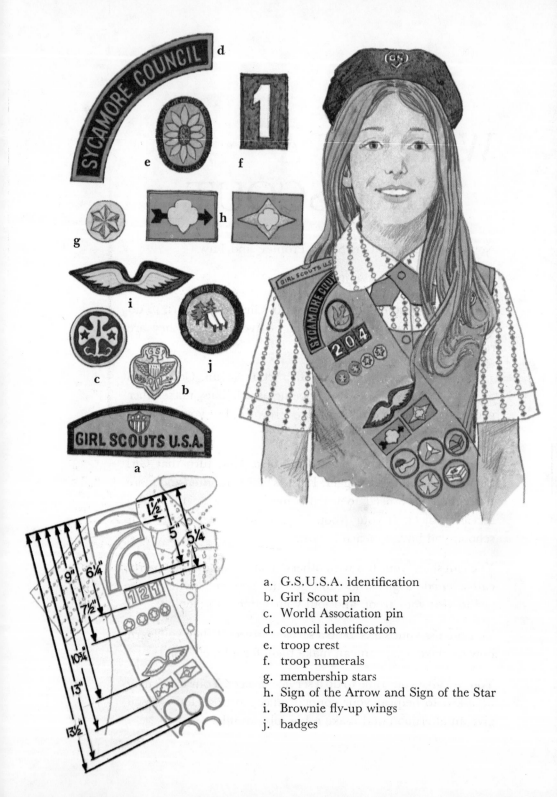

a. G.S.U.S.A. identification
b. Girl Scout pin
c. World Association pin
d. council identification
e. troop crest
f. troop numerals
g. membership stars
h. Sign of the Arrow and Sign of the Star
i. Brownie fly-up wings
j. badges

The Girl Scout UNIFORM can be worn only by Girl Scouts who are registered and have a membership card. The way you act when you wear your uniform shows that you really mean your Girl Scout Promise. You are proud of your uniform, so you keep it neat and clean. You may wear a watch, ring, or religious medals with your uniform but no other jewelry—not even Girl Scout jewelry. You can buy your uniform at a Girl Scout shop or by mail from Girl Scout National Equipment Service.

Most insignia go on your badge sash. Look at the sash in the picture to see where to sew or pin each piece of insignia. You wear your sash as soon as you become a Junior Girl Scout. You add to it insignia you earn as a Junior. When you are a Cadette Scout, you add Cadette insignia. You leave room under your membership stars for Cadette insignia. You earn one membership star for each year you are a Girl Scout. Membership stars are on colored circles—green for Brownie, yellow for Junior, white for Cadette, red for Senior.

The GIRL SCOUT PIN has the shape of a trefoil. "Trefoil" means three leaves. The three leaves of the pin stand for the three parts of the Promise—On my honor, I will try:

> To serve God.
> My country and mankind.
> And to live by the Girl Scout Law.

When your leader pins you, you become a Junior Girl Scout. Cadette Scouts, Senior Scouts, and troop leaders wear this same pin. You can wear it on everyday clothes.

The Girl Scout SIGN is made with three fingers, which stand for the three parts of the Promise. You give the sign when you say your Promise. You give the sign to your leader when she invests you as a Girl Scout. The Girl Scout sign is a way to say "hi" to a Scout on the street or wherever you meet. If you see a Scout or Guide from another country and give the sign, she will know you are a Scout, too.

The Girl Scout HANDSHAKE is a special way to greet another Scout. You shake with your left hand so you can give the Girl Scout sign with your right hand. Girl Scouts often use this handshake at ceremonies when they receive a pin or badge.

The friends of a Girl Scout are all the Girl Scouts and Girl Guides around the world. These girls make the same Promise you make and follow the same Law, though they use different words. They are called "Girl Guides" in Canada— "Gaaru Sukauto" in Japan—"Guias" in Mexico—"Eclaireuses" in France— "Flickscouts" in Sweden—"Mursheda" in Sudan—"Pfadfinderin" in Switzerland —and many other names.

They wear different uniforms and pins, but a trefoil is always part of their pin. They all have troops and patrols and use the same sign and handshake you use.

The WORLD ASSOCIATION PIN is the badge of the World Association of Girl Guides and Girl Scouts. You wear this pin and so do all the Girl Guides and Girl Scouts from other countries. This pin has a special meaning just as your Girl Scout pin has. The blue stands for the sky and the gold stands for the sun. The trefoil stands for the three parts of the Promise. The base of the trefoil is shaped like a flame and this stands for the love of mankind and the flame that burns in the hearts of Girl Guides and Girl Scouts around the world. The line in the middle of the trefoil stands for the compass needle that guides us. The two stars stand for the Promise and Law.

Switzerland

Japan

Sudan

Canada

15

HOW SCOUTING BEGAN

Robert Baden-Powell lived in England. When he was a boy, he loved to camp out in all sorts of weather. He trained himself to walk in the woods without making a sound. He discovered the ways of animals and birds.

When he grew up, he became an officer in the British army. The scouting skills he learned as a boy helped to make him an excellent soldier. One year he was sent to India. The soldiers in his troop did not know how to live in the out-of-doors and scout in the woods. So Baden-Powell decided to teach them. He divided the men into small groups called patrols. He invented games to make them fend for themselves. He taught the patrol leaders how to lead their patrols.

When Robert Baden-Powell returned to England, he found out that the boys at home wanted to play the games of scouting, too. So he wrote a book called *Scouting for Boys*. In 1909 all the Boy Scouts came to a big meeting in London. But they did not come alone. A party of girls marched with the boys. If boys could be Scouts, the girls said, why couldn't they?

And so Baden-Powell started the Girl Guides in England. His sister, Agnes Baden-Powell, became the first President.

Soon boys and girls all over the world wanted Scouting and Guiding, too. Robert Baden-Powell and his wife Olave trav-

eled to many countries and helped start Scouting and Guiding. Baden-Powell was honored by the King of England for his Boy Scout work and after that he was called Lord Baden-Powell. He was elected Chief Scout of the World, and Lady Baden-Powell was made World Chief Guide.

One of Lord and Lady Baden-Powell's friends was an American named Juliette Gordon Low. Everyone called her by her nickname, Daisy. She was born in Savannah, Georgia in 1860. Her father had been born in Georgia, too, but her mother was born in Chicago when that big city was a small frontier village.

During the Civil War, Daisy's family moved to Chicago to live with Grandfather Kinzie, a government agent for the Indians. Sometimes Daisy would look out the window to see Indians camping in her grandfather's yard.

After the war, the Gordons moved back to Savannah, and Daisy organized her first club. She named it "Helpful Hands" and its purpose, of course, was to help. But alas—the club's very first job went wrong. The club planned to sew clothes for a poor family. But Daisy Gordon didn't know much about sewing. The clothes fell apart almost as soon as they were finished. "Helpful Hands" became known as "Helpless Hands."

But Daisy learned many things well—especially drawing. Her parents were proud when she earned good marks at school.

Daisy Gordon married William Low, a handsome young Englishman, and went with him to live in England. When he died, Daisy Gordon Low traveled in Europe, to India, to Egypt.

Then, in England, she met Baden-Powell. He asked Daisy Low to become a Girl Guide leader. She did and led three Girl Guide troops in Scotland and England. Then she returned home . . . with a dream.

The moment Daisy reached her home in Savannah, she telephoned a friend. "Come right over, Nina," she said excitedly. "I've got something for the girls of Savannah, and all America, and all the world, and we're going to start it tonight!"

The first Girl Guide company was organized on March 12, 1912 in Savannah. The first camp was held the next summer. And that year the girls voted to change the name from Girl Guides to Girl Scouts.

By this time Daisy Low was almost totally deaf. Yet nothing could stop her. All over the United States she traveled, sharing her ideas, starting Girl Scout troops.

Millions of girls have made the Girl Scout Promise since then. And the Girl Scout Promise *you* make is the very promise Daisy Low made to herself when she first brought Girl Scouting to America, over fifty years ago.

GIRL SCOUT DAYS

GIRL SCOUT BIRTHDAY March 12

The first Girl Scout troop meeting was on March 12, 1912. Every year Girl Scouts celebrate that day with parties and special ceremonies or service projects.

JULIETTE LOW'S BIRTHDAY October 31

The Founder of the Girl Scouts in the United States was born on Halloween in 1860. Girl Scouts celebrate her birthday in many special ways.

THINKING DAY February 22

One day each year Girl Guides and Girl Scouts everywhere join their thoughts and send them round the world as a powerful prayer that all men shall be friends. They chose February 22 as the day to do this because it is the birthday of both Lord and Lady Baden-Powell.

THINKING DAY FUND

People also give presents on birthdays. So in every country Girl Scouts and Girl Guides give money to the Thinking Day Fund. The Fund is used to start Girl Scout troops in countries where people need help.

JULIETTE LOW WORLD FRIENDSHIP FUND

Juliette Low wished Girl Scouts could know Guides and Scouts in other countries. Girl Scouts in the U.S.A. give money to the Juliette Low World Friendship Fund to help make that wish come true. Part of the money is sent to the Thinking Day Fund. Part of it is used to send Girl Scouts to other countries, and to bring Girl Guides from other countries here. When you give your money to this Fund, you help bring together people from different lands so they can become friends.

BADGES

There are over 40 badges that Junior Scouts can earn; each badge is about a different subject. So you can have lots to choose from. You can even make up a badge of your own!

Each badge has its own "requirements." These are things you will need to do to earn the badge. Each requirement is a way to find out about, to try or to practice something about the subject you have chosen. With your troop leader's help, you can change some badge requirements, if you want to make the badge more fun or more useful to you.

Most often, you work on badges with a small group of friends who are all interested in the same badge subject. Sometimes you earn a badge that no one else has chosen. Visiting different places, making things, meeting people, teaching others what you have learned—all can be part of the fun of earning a badge.

For each badge you earn, there is a badge symbol you can wear on your uniform sash. It shows that you have new knowledge and skills that you can use and share with others!

Keep a record of your badge work by having your leader (or another person chosen by you and your leader) fill in the blank beside each requirement as soon as you finish it. You may do part of a badge at camp. You might even move to another place and another troop before you complete a badge. If you keep a record in this book, you and your leader will know which requirements you have done. You and your troop leader decide when you have earned a badge. When you have done each requirement and can meet the purpose, you have earned the badge.

Badges are presented at a ceremony called COURT OF AWARDS. Then you sew your badges on your badge sash. Your troop may want to have a Court of Awards as soon as most of the girls have earned their first badge. Or you may wait and have a big Court of Awards and have all the badges earned by the troop presented and invite guests.

What do these badges stand for?

21

SOME STEPS YOU CAN TAKE TO CHOOSE AND EARN BADGES

1. **Pick a subject** that interests you—one that is new to you or one that you would like to learn more about.

2. **Look through** pages 318-365 to find badges with activities about your subject.

→ **Can't find badges covering your subject?**

If you and others in your troop have an interest that the badges don't cover, you can create a new badge of your own.
  For "how to," see page 364.

3. **When you find some badges** that fit your interest:
   - Read the badge purpose and requirements carefully
   - Choose the badges you would like to earn and decide which ones you want to do first.

4. **Seek out others** in the troop who would like to earn the same badges as those you have chosen.

→ **No one else shares your interest?**

Ask your leader if you can work **on your own.**

5. **With your leader's help:**
   - Join forces with girls who want to earn the same badge.
   - Get an adviser who will help you as you earn this badge.
     - your troop leader?
     - a parent or teacher?
     - a Cadette or Senior Scout?
     - someone else?

6. **Talk over:**
   - How do the badge requirements help me meet the purpose of the badge?
   - Which requirements sound like fun?
   - Do any requirements sound dull or boring? Which ones? Why?
   - What are some interesting ways to do each requirement?

7. **Then decide:**
   - Which requirements will be done as written in the Handbook?
   - Will I (we) rewrite any requirements? Which ones? Why?
   - Should any requirements be dropped? Why?
   - Will I (we) add any requirements? What will they be?
   - What are my goals, and how will I know when I have successfully earned the badge?

EARN YOUR BADGE!

PATHS TO ACTION

A Junior Girl Scout may earn the Sign of the Arrow and the Sign of the Star. Each of the two Junior Scout signs is an invitation to action! A badge is about one subject, while a sign includes *many different* subjects to explore.

Signs, too, have requirements to help you get started and learn about the things that interest you. For some parts of a sign, you might earn a badge. For other parts, you might help carry out another kind of project, such as making your own film, going on a trip, or doing something for your community.

Each sign has its own symbol that you can wear on your uniform sash as a reminder of your adventures and accomplishments.

Sign of the Arrow

The arrow with the trefoil on it says, "This is the way," on the path of Girl Scouting.

The Sign of the Arrow is a symbol of direction and discovery! It gives you, as a Girl Scout, the chance to find and follow many paths to fun, learning, and adventure. A girl wearing the Sign of the Arrow has gained new skills and can set new directions for herself.

Each sign activity points the way for you to become more "on your own," making your ideas and abilities count by choosing and carrying out projects you would like to do, by yourself and with others. You'll reach out, finding new interests and stretching your imagination by sharing things you already enjoy, and tackling new things you want to try for the first time. All along the way, you'll be learning and using new skills to help yourself, your friends, your family, and community.

Four big signposts mark starting points for your adventures. You create your own paths by choosing and completing two activities in each of the big action areas.

You can do sign activities in any order, and in many different ways, working at troop meetings, at home, at camp, or in your community.

You may want to earn some badges while working on the sign. To do this, you can pick the activities that say, "earn a badge." Or you might decide to earn a badge as your way of carrying out one of the other projects.

The paths you follow may be different from anyone else's, since you choose the activities that are most interesting to you and figure out how you will do them. When you have completed activities along every path, you can receive the Sign of the Arrow as a bright sign of your accomplishment.

Going Places

Around the corner or around the globe, the world is filled with interesting things and people. You can open the doors of discovery with a little curiosity and alertness.

Test your know-how for finding your way by doing at least two of these activities.

Take a trip with friends or family to some place near or far— some place you have never been before. Help decide where and how to go and what you will see and do there and on the way.

Keep some kind of log or record of your trip that you can save and share with others. Include your thoughts and feelings about what you saw and did.

I visited_____on_____

I went with_____

OR

Earn a badge that helps you learn something you can use during hikes, camping, or other outdoor activities, or for exploring your community.

Decide Guide: What would you like to learn?

What badges might help you learn these things?

I earned the_____badge,

because_____

_____

The most interesting thing I learned_____

OR

Lead your own guided tour of a place you enjoy and know well.

Decide Guide: Where will you go on your tour?

Whom will you take?

What will you show and tell them?

When and how will you do this?

I led a tour to_____

Whom I took on the tour_____

_____

OR

Take part in a project that helps you learn something about girls and boys your age who live in another part of your community, another part of the U.S.A., or another part of the world.

Decide Guide: Whom do you want to learn about?

What do you want to find out?

What kind of project could help you find out what you want to know?

Whom I learned about_____

_____

The kind of project I took part in_____

OR

Create and carry out your own *Going Places* project, different from any of these—a project you design to help you explore your special interests in people and places.

The project I (we) created_____

_____

Some discoveries I (we) made_____

Making Things Happen

Putting ideas in action is what Making Things Happen is all about. And working with others to make your ideas reality is how it's done. Have the fun of sharing and learning as you make your ideas count.

Do at least two of these activities.

With your patrol or others in your troop, plan and rehearse an entertainment that you could put on at short notice. Choose an audience and put on your entertainment, then be ready to perform again if you should be asked!

Our entertainment was about_____

It was held at_____on_____

We put on our entertainment for_____

and again for_____

OR

Help plan and carry out a skills day, play day, or song festival.

Decide Guide: When and where will you hold it?

What games, songs, or activities will you include?

Who will be invited and how will you invite them?

How much will your program cost?

How will you pay for your program?

We held a_____

that took place on_____

Whom we invited_____

OR

With others in your troop, choose a subject you want to learn more about. Invite someone who is an expert on that subject to visit and teach you some of the things you want to know about or learn to do.

Decide Guide: What interests you most?

Whom will you invite?

What will you ask this person to do?

When and how will you invite your guest?

The subject we chose was_____

We invited_____

who is an expert on_____

What we most enjoyed doing_____

_____

_____

Some things we learned by carrying out our project_____

_____

_____

OR

With two or three friends, invent something that can be used and enjoyed by all members of your troop—a secret code, a game, or anything else you think they could use or would enjoy. When your invention is completed, share it with the troop and tell them how each inventor helped create it.

28

We invented_____

I helped by_____

OR

With others, create and carry out a special *Making Things Happen* project that is different from any of these—a project that helps you and your friends put your own ideas into action and make them count.

The project we created_____

What we made happen_____

Building Friendships

Help yourself discover more about making, keeping, and being a friend.

Do at least two of these activities.

Reach out to make a new friend by getting acquainted with someone whom you would like to be friends with. Together, do some things that help you and your new friend get to know each other better.

Decide Guide: Whom would you like to be friends with?

What interests do you share and what new things could you learn?

What kinds of things would be fun for you and your new friend to do together?

My new friend is_____

How we first met_____

OR

Help plan and take part in a project that helps Brownie Scouts learn something about being a Friend Maker.

Our project was_____

What I helped the Brownies learn_____

What I learned about making friends_____

OR

Design and make a gift that someone you know could use and would enjoy. It might be for a friend your age, or for an adult who is important to you.

I decided to make_____

for_____

because_____

OR

Help a friend do something that he or she thinks is very important.

I helped my friend to_____

How I helped my friend_____

OR

Create and carry out your own special *Building Friendships* project, different from any of these—a project that helps you make new friends or strengthen old friendships.

The project I created_____

What I learned about friendship_____

30

Helping Your Community

Simply by living in a community makes you a citizen. By actively involving yourself in its problems and projects you have an effect on the kind of place your community is. Try making yourself count as a citizen.

Do at least two of these activities.

Make up a game to help people learn interesting things about your community. Teach your game to as many different people as you can.

My game helps people learn more about_____
_____

I shared my game with_____
_____

OR

Help create and carry out a project that demonstrates how Girl Scouting helps your community.

Decide Guide: What do people in your community already know about Girl Scouting, and what more would you like them to know?

What are some ways you can show how Girl Scouts help as citizens of their community?

Whom I worked with_____

What we did_____

OR

Help a community group or organization that is doing something to improve your town. Use your skills to carry out some part of their effort.

Decide Guide: What are some community projects girls your age might help with?

What kinds of help can you offer?

How will you arrange to take part in a project you choose?

The group I helped_____

How I helped_____

_____

Some things I learned about being an active citizen_____

_____

_____

OR

Develop and carry out your own special *Helping Your Community* project that is different from any of these—a project that involves you in your community.

The project I (we) developed_____

_____

What I (we) learned about community action_____

_____

_____

OR

Earn a badge that helps you learn something about being a good citizen in your home, in your troop, in your school, or in your neighborhood.

Decide Guide: What do you think a good citizen needs to know and do?

What badges might help you learn or do some of these things?

I learned the_____badge

because_____

Sign of the Star

*A star shines in all directions
and guides you along the way.*

Exploring, seeking, and testing are all important parts of the Sign of the Star. Earning this sign helps you look at yourself, other people, and the world in new ways. You are called upon to act on your new discoveries to help your world and to become the kind of person you would like to be.

Each sign activity is a call to action and adventure, inviting you to explore your thoughts, feelings, and talents! You will find ways to have fun and help others, ways to make friends and learn new things that are important to you, and ways to discover the what's and why's of your special interests. As you carry out the sign activities, you'll be testing your skills, your understanding, and your abilities in ways you choose.

The Sign of the Star activities are built around six Action Calls. You can do the activities in any order and in many different ways. Parts of some projects you can do alone, but for some you will need to work with others.

With your troop leader's help, you and your troopmates choose, plan, and carry out each project. Meet every Call to Action and you can proudly say, "I have earned the Sign of the Star."

ACTION CALL

Discovering You

Most everyone is interested in how things work: why it rains, how an engine runs, or what makes an animated character move around a screen. To find out, you can read and ask questions, but often the best way to understand something is to experience it. The same is true when it comes to understanding the way you work. Self-discovery can often be as simple as taking a step back and watching yourself in action.

Do at least two of these activities to help discover more about yourself.

Teach someone else how to do something that you can do well—something that would be useful or enjoyable to the other person.

OR

List three or four things that are especially hard for you to do, and choose the one most important to you right now. Find some ways to learn to do it better.

OR

Create something that tells others about yourself. You might make a painting, collage, or photo collection, write an original story or poem, or do something different from any of these ideas. Make your choice, carry it out, and share your original creation with your family and troop.

OR

Invent some ways to become a better friend, student, or family member. Test your ideas and, if you aren't satisfied, make changes to improve your plan. Invent an interesting way to share your discoveries with your troop.

Explore: Who and what is important to me?

What can I do well?

What would I like to learn, try, or practice?

Seek: In what ways can I share my knowledge, skills, and talents?

People, places, things to do that can help me learn something.

Test: How well can I use what I know to help myself?

How well can I use what I know to help other people?

33a

ACTION CALL

Getting Things Done with Others

Experience the feeling of team spirit and accomplishment that comes from working with others to choose and reach a common goal.

Do any one of these activities.

With a group, create your own newspaper. Name it and share the responsibility among yourselves for gathering information, putting it all together, and getting it to your readers.

OR

With others in your troop, create your own Our Own Troop's Badge. (See page 346 for directions.)

OR

With others, choose, plan, and carry out three "Secret Good Turns" for someone else.

OR

With members of your family, choose, plan, and carry out a special project that all of you would like to do together.

Explore: What actually happens when a group of people plans and carries out a project together?

What was easy and fun about it?

What was difficult about it?

Seek: Ways of choosing and planning that are fun for everyone in the group.

A project that we will be proud of.

Test: How well can I work as a member of a group to get something done?

How can I use what I learn to plan and carry out other projects?

33b

ACTION CALL
Improving Your Community

City or suburb, town or country village, your community—
like your troop—is only as great as you make it. As a citizen,
you have responsibility for your community, as do your
parents and others younger and older than yourself. Look
around. Are there things that need doing? Be an active citizen.
Don't wait for someone else to get things going—make your
move!

With your patrol or another group, choose, plan, and carry
out a project to help make your community a better place in
which to live.

Explore: What is "best" about our community?

How do people live, work, and grow in it?

How could it be improved?

How can we find out about these things?

Seek: What are the most useful things we can do for our
community?

What are some ways of doing these things?

Who can help us carry out our plans?

What skills do we need to carry out our plans?

Test: How well can we plan together?

What happened as a result of our efforts?

Was our project a success, or could it have been
more effective?

What changes would we make if we did it again,
and what would we do the same?

ACTION CALL
Communicating

Words, pictures, and movements are a few of the many means of communicating. Even when you don't realize it, you are sending out and receiving messages.

Increase your knowledge and skill in communicating by doing at least two of these activities.

Make up your own play, comic strip, chart, movie, or filmstrip about troop government and how it works. Present and discuss this with a group of Brownie Girl Scouts, younger or new Junior Scouts.

OR

Meet with a girl your own age who is a member of an ethnic, racial, or religious group different from your own. With her, develop a project or activities that you can do together to help each of you learn more about your likenesses and differences.

OR

Go on a silent communications search. Explore some ways that people can "talk" to each other about themselves and about ideas and feeling *without using words!* Try some ways of silent communication yourself and share your discoveries with your family or troop in some interesting way.

Explore: How do people communicate with others?

Seek: In what ways can I sharpen my skills of communicating ideas, thoughts, and feelings?

What happens when people can communicate with each other?

What happens when people can't communicate with each other?

Test: How well can I communicate with people older and younger, similar and different from myself?

ACTION CALL
Being Creative

Cooking a tasty meal, solving a problem, or organizing an enjoyable project—creativity is an important part of so many things. By pooling your experience, imagination, and ingenuity with others, you can combine ideas to come up with something that is new and exciting.

With others, make up a Wide Game* that can help the members of your troop discover more about each of these things:
listening and observing
solving a problem
creating a story, skit, picture, or poem

Explore: Why do people like to play games?

What makes a game interesting? exciting? dull? useful?

Seek: What kinds of activities help people learn more about how to listen? to solve problems? to use their skills and talents?

How do we go about planning an activity for someone else to do? What things do we have to think about?

Test: Can we put our ideas together so that our game is fun for everyone?

What did we learn by planning the game?

What do we think others learned by playing the game?

*For ways to create a Wide Game see p. 162, or p. 174 of the *Cadette Girl Scout Handbook*, and *Games for Girl Scouts*.

ACTION CALL
Choosing Ideals

Everyone chooses ideals to live up to. Where do ideals and values come from, and how do you decide which ones are important to you?

Begin your own ideals quest by doing at least two of these activities.

Start a collection of pictures, stories, and poems that tells about the different ideals and values that people have and about how they try to live up to those ideals in their daily lives.

OR

Create a Scouts' Own play, TV show, film, or filmstrip about the Girl Scout Promise and Law and what they mean to you.

OR

Choose two or three people in your community whom you admire—people living by ideals you think are important. Plan and carry out an interview with one of these people. Decide what questions you will ask in the interview and how you will record the conversation.

Explore: What are some examples of ideals and values?

How do people express their ideals and values?

Seek: What is important to me?

What are my ideals?

How are they different from or similar to ideals of other people?

Test: How well do I act on what I believe?

How can I live up to my highest ideals?

PATROL SYSTEM

COURT OF HONOR

PATROL

A Girl Scout troop belongs to all its members. The troop decides what it will do, and every girl helps to carry out the troop's decisions. That is another way of saying that a Girl Scout troop is a democracy.

In a democracy each person can say what he wants the government to do, and he can vote for what he wants. Then, when a decision has been made, he does his part to carry it out. This is the way citizens help to run their country. This is the way Girl Scouts help to run their troop.

The government of Girl Scout troops is called the patrol system. It is made up of patrols and a Court of Honor. This is the system started by Lord Baden-Powell in India when he first taught his young soldiers scouting. Now it is used by all Girl Scouts, Girl Guides, and Boy Scouts throughout the world.

39

ballot   voice   show of hands

Patrols

To start the patrol system, your troop first decides how to divide up into small groups. You might have five or six or eight girls in each group. These small groups are called patrols.

Suppose your troop has thirty girls. You might have five patrols with six girls in each. Or suppose your troop has only twenty girls. Then you might have two patrols with seven girls in each and one with six. Or you might have four patrols with five girls in each. Your leader will help you decide how many girls should be in each patrol.

Next, decide which girls will be in each patrol. Here are two ways:

* Each girl in the troop writes the names of three other girls whom she would like to be with in a patrol. Then your troop leader forms patrols based on girls' choices. Each patrol elects its own leaders.

* Each girl draws from a hat a slip of paper which stands for one of the patrols. Then each patrol elects its own leader.

Scout vote

Each patrol should have an assistant patrol leader. The patrol leader may pick a girl to be assistant patrol leader, or the whole patrol may elect an assistant.

The patrol leader stays in office until the whole troop decides it is time to elect new patrol leaders or to make new patrols. This term of office may be as short as two or three months, when a troop has just started using patrols. In troops with more patrol experience, the term of office may be six months.

When your troop is divided into patrols, each patrol holds a meeting in a separate corner of the troop meeting place.

The patrol leader is in charge of the meeting. She writes down the name, address, and telephone number of each patrol member. She uses that list of names to take attendance at each meeting and to collect weekly dues.

Each patrol will want to choose a name. Probably every girl will have a favorite. So the patrol leader asks the patrol members for suggestions, and then all vote for the one they like best. The patrol leader counts the votes. The name that gets the most votes wins.

41

A secret patrol signal can be decided in the same way. Maybe one girl wants the signal to be a whistle. But other girls want the signal to be a clap or a call. After each patrol member has given her idea, all vote for the signal they like best.

Next, the patrol may decide to vote for a patrol flag. Ideas for a flag will have to be drawn on paper by each patrol member, but you vote on the drawings just as you voted on names and signals.

In your "patrol corner" you practice making a bedroll, knots, first aid. You learn songs and games.

Patrols take turns carrying out a part of the troop meeting. At the Court of Honor the patrol leader finds out what her patrol's part is.

Court of Honor

The Court of Honor makes plans and decisions for the whole troop just as patrol members make plans and decisions for their patrol. All the patrol leaders plus the troop scribe and the troop treasurer and the troop leader are members of the Court of Honor.

The Court of Honor decides what each patrol will do for the next troop meeting.

The Court of Honor makes suggestions for patrols to vote on.

The Court of Honor asks patrols for suggestions.

troop leader

patrol leaders

troop scribe

The Court of Honor

troop treasurer

Your patrol leader speaks for you and other patrol members at the Court of Honor. The other patrol leaders speak for their patrol members. So, in a way everybody is a member of the Court of Honor. But instead of all the troop members being there in person—which would make too much of a crowd—they are *represented* by their patrol leaders. That is why this system is called *representative democracy*. It is the same system that our country uses. Instead of all the people in the country going to Washington, D.C. to run their government, they elect the President and Congressmen to represent them.

When the Court of Honor plans several weeks ahead, it makes a kaper chart showing what each patrol must do. Then the troop leader gives the patrol leaders tips on how to carry out their part.

KAPER CHART FOR SEPTEMBER TROOP MEETINGS

	SEPT 7	SEPT 14	SEPT 21	SEPT 28
CLOSING FOR TROOP MEETING (CHOOSE AND CARRY OUT)	✳	6	ϟ	Ω
PUT CHAIRS AND SUPPLIES AWAY AT END OF MEETING	Ω	✳	6	ϟ
GAME TO PLAY DURING MEETING	ϟ	Ω	✳	6
SURPRISE! YOU MAY BE ASKED TO HELP OR DO SOMETHING THIS WEEK OR YOU MAY HAVE A "FREE" WEEK.	6	ϟ	Ω	✳

✳ SHOOTING STAR   ϟ LIGHTNING PATROL
6 SNAPPY 6   Ω HORSESHOE PATROL

Your patrol leader reports to your patrol what it must do to get ready for future meetings. Suppose most of the patrols voted for a Valentine's Day party, and your patrol is in charge of the heart cookies. You have to decide who will get the recipe, who will get the flour and sugar and other ingredients, who will get the heart cookie cutters, and whose kitchen you will use to bake in. Then you make a kaper chart. Your patrol will have to have its own meeting at a troop member's house when you bake the cookies.

KAPERS FOR EAGER EIGHT PATROL	
MAKE COOKIES. EVERYBODY TAKE A TURN MIXING OR CUTTING OR DECORATING THE COOKIES, THEN CLEAN UP.	
SCRAPE AND STACK THE BOWLS, SPOONS, CUPS — READY FOR WASHING	LINDA AND KIM
WASH COOKING UTENSILS	BETTY JEAN AND LAURIE
WIPE TABLE TOPS	CONNIE
PUT EVERYTHING AWAY	JEANNE AND PAT
SWEEP THE FLOOR	KATHY

Sometimes the Court of Honor will have ideas for things to do, and your patrol leader will ask you to vote on the ideas. After you have voted, she will report your decision to the Court of Honor.

When the Court of Honor asks for suggestions, your patrol leader reports your ideas. The other patrol leaders report the ideas of their patrols. The troop scribe makes a list in her notebook. The Court of Honor then works with ideas from all the patrols.

The Court of Honor holds a short meeting either before or after every troop meeting. But sometimes the Court of Honor may decide to have a long meeting to plan a big project. A long meeting is held on a different day from the troop meeting. It may be in the regular meeting place or in the troop leader's home or in some other place that is convenient.

Sometimes the entire troop may want to discuss something together, instead of by patrols. You can still do this. The Court of Honor decides what is best to discuss in patrols and what may be better for the entire troop to talk over together.

A patrol is as good as each girl in it. Your job as a patrol member is to tell your ideas, to vote, and to carry out your part of patrol plans. Your patrol leader depends on you.

PATROL LEADER

A patrol leader wears a gold patrol leader cord over her left shoulder. Her job is fun but it is also a responsibility. A patrol leader must be fair, friendly, and helpful and have good ideas for things to do. She reports all her patrol members' ideas to the Court of Honor, even the ones she doesn't like. And when she reports back to her patrol from the Court of Honor, she must be fair and give each girl in the patrol a chance to speak. A patrol leader must see that things get done, but she must not do everything herself.

ASSISTANT PATROL LEADER

The assistant helps the patrol leader in every way she can. The patrol leader may ask her to take attendance and collect dues every week. Or she may be patrol song or game leader. She takes charge of the patrol when the patrol leader is absent. She represents the patrol at the Court of Honor if the patrol leader is not there. She may be invited to attend Court of Honor even when the patrol leader is there.

TROOP SCRIBE AND TROOP TREASURER

The whole troop votes for a scribe and a treasurer to go to the Court of Honor and to do these special jobs: The troop scribe writes letters for the troop and keeps a notebook for the Court of Honor. The troop treasurer receives the weekly dues from patrol leaders and works with the troop leader to keep a record in the troop record book of how dues are spent. The troop decides how many months the scribe and treasurer serve before new ones are elected.

RULES OF ORDER
FOR MEETINGS

Certain rules have been made up for running any kind of business meeting. Similar rules are used in the United States Congress and in your parents' club meetings. You can use them in your troop meetings when there is business to be done by the entire troop.

The person in charge of the meeting is called "the chairman" or "the chair" for short. The chairman starts the meeting.

Chairman: "The meeting will please come to order. The Court of Honor has had suggestions that our troop buy a pack basket to carry food to the cookout and a dozen pairs of scissors to make oven mitts with. We only have enough money in the troop treasury for either the basket or the scissors. Is there a motion on how to spend the money we have?"

Carol has her hand up first, so the chair calls on her.

Chairman: "I recognize Carol."

Then Carol can talk, and no one else can.

Carol: "I move that the troop buy a pack basket."

When an idea is said that way, it is called a "motion." In order to be sure that at least one other person likes the idea, every motion must be "seconded."

Sandy wants the troop to buy the pack basket, too, so she raises her hand. When the chairman recognizes her, she can speak.

Sandy:	"I second the motion."
Chairman:	"The motion has been made by Carol and seconded by Sandy. Is there any discussion?"

Any troop member who wants to say something about the idea raises her hand and is recognized. When there are no more hands raised, the chairman calls for a vote.

Chairman:	"The motion is that the troop buy a pack basket. All in favor say Aye."

All the troop members who want to buy the basket answer in a loud voice.

All:	"Aye!"
Chairman:	"All opposed say No."

All the troop members who would rather buy the scissors instead of the basket answer in a loud voice.

All:	"No!"

If the chairman is sure from the sound whether there are more Ayes or more Noes, she announces the vote.

Chairman:	"The Ayes have it. The motion is carried."

or

"The Noes have it. The motion is defeated."

Sometimes, when the vote is very close, the chairman may ask the girls to vote again by showing hands.

After the vote, the chairman goes on to the next motion. When all the business is finished, the chairman ends the meeting.

Chairman:	"The meeting is adjourned."

GIRL SCOUT TROOP 91

TROOP MONEY

Your troop will need money to carry out some plans. The money your troop spends comes from the troop treasury, and the money that fills the treasury comes from troop dues. Dues are paid by troop members at each meeting. The troop decides how much dues will be.

There may be a time when your troop will plan something that costs much more money than there is in the troop treasury. A camping trip perhaps. Then you will need a troop money-earning project. Your troop leader will have ideas for this.

Keeping a record of how much money you collect and how much you spend is important, so you know how much money you have. Dues collected are recorded in the troop record book by the troop treasurer. The treasurer and the troop leader deposit the money in a bank under your troop's name. When troop money is spent, a record is made in the troop record book. The girl who spends the money reports what she bought and the cost to the troop treasurer, who puts it in the record book.

Members of your troop can take turns shopping for troop supplies. Several Scouts can go together, or you may want to go with your mother or an adult. Before you go, be sure you know how much you need to buy and how you are going to use your supplies. The first time you shop, you may have one or two things on your list. The next time your list may be longer.

After girls have had turns shopping and putting down how much things cost, your troop can make a budget. A troop budget is a plan for how money will be spent. You need a budget when you plan something that costs more than one week's dues.

How do you make a budget? You put down the money you expect to spend and beside that the money you expect to have. This shows whether you have enough money for your trip or party.

Here is a sample budget for a cookout. There are thirty girls in this troop. Dues are 10 cents a week, so they collect $3 each week.

BUDGET FOR A COOKOUT

INCOME		EXPENSES	
Money left in treasury	$ 6.00	Bus fare to park and back (20¢ each x 30 girls)	$ 6.00
May dues ($3.00 x 4 weeks)	12.00	Food for cookout	15.00
Total	$18.00	Total	$21.00

hamburger
chili beans
tomato sauce
crackers
punch mix
total $15.00

This troop needs $21, but by the end of May they will have only $18. They will have to change their plan. They can spend less on food or each girl can bring her own carfare. Or they can wait another week until they have the $21 they need.

When your troop wants to do something that costs much more than your troop income for one month, figure how long it takes to save that much money. Make a budget for that much time.

Sometimes a Court of Honor makes budgets. They present the budget to the troop and members can ask questions about it.

GOING PLACES

Going some place with your troop is fun and it is a good way to find out things. When you go some place, you can see for yourself. You can watch. You can listen and smell and touch.

When you come back you can tell about what you saw. Maybe you will want to know even more. Then you can read more about it and ask more questions.

Where To Go

Your patrol voted to take a trip. Now your patrol leader wants ideas for places to go.

What do you like? What would you like to know more about?

* Animals and birds are found at the zoo, on a farm, in the woods, in a pet shop.
* Fish swim in an aquarium, a pond.
* Stars can be seen from an observatory or a hillside on a clear night.
* Flowers grow in parks and greenhouses and flower stores and people's gardens.
* Trees stand in parks and woods and some young trees are in tree nurseries.

There are other places to go. Museums show how girls lived long ago or what a town was like. Exhibits show how things happen, what is new.

What would you like to watch?

* Trains come in at the railroad station.

* Ships and ferries dock at the waterfront.

* Airplanes land at the airport.

* Buildings are being built or torn down somewhere in the city.

* Fruits and vegetables come to the market by trucks from the country.

* Ice cream is made in a dairy and cakes are made in a bakery.

Sometimes you go back to a place you have been to before. That is a good idea. Then you see things you did not notice the first time.

Getting Ready

You know where you are going to go.

Now you get ready.

You think about what you are going to do on your trip, what you need to bring, who should know about it.

Find out how to get there. Maybe you can walk. Can you go one way and come back another way? Maybe you will take a bus. What time will it leave? When will it come back? As you walk along sidewalks or board buses will the whole troop make too big a group? Maybe it will be easier to travel by patrols.

Decide what to wear and what to bring with you. Will you wear your uniform? Will you need especially warm clothing or rain boots? Do you plan to cook? Then you will need some equipment. Decide what you will need and which girl will bring it. Decide who will bring the first aid kit.

Add together all the money you will need
—bus fare . . . admission . . . food. How
will your troop get the money? Is there
enough in the troop treasury? Or should
each girl bring her own carfare and the
treasury pay for everything else?

Investigate the place you are going to
visit. What is the best time to be there?
Do you need to make a reservation or ask
for permission to come? Will someone be
there to answer questions? The more you
know about what you are going to see
before you go, the more you will see when
you are there.

Will rain change your plans? Make a plan
to use in case of rain.

Know what your part of the trip is. What
are you supposed to bring or find out?

Tell your parents all about the trip plans,
and get their permission to go on the trip.

On the Trip

There are certain ways to act on a trip that make traveling much nicer for everybody. When you act this way with your troop or your family, you are carrying out the Girl Scout Laws, and you are a good traveler.

Some of the Girl Scout Laws you carry out are: A Girl Scout's honor is to be trusted; A Girl Scout is courteous; A Girl Scout is kind to animals; A Girl Scout obeys orders; A Girl Scout is cheerful; A Girl Scout is clean in thought, word, and deed.

Girl Scout ways to act on a trip:

* Keep inside the car, or bus or train. Keep your hands, your head, even your elbow inside the window.

* Walk along the left side of the road with cars coming *toward* you—not behind you. Walk single file or by twos. Obey all the signs. Cross only where signs say you may.

* If you must walk along a road after dark, wear something white or carry a flashlight so that drivers can see you.

* Never accept or ask for rides from strangers.

* Stay with your buddy and your group. Remember where you decided to meet if you get lost.

* Be courteous to other people in a bus or train or along a sidewalk. Save your songs and games for the right time and place. Be cheerful when you have to wait your turn in a restaurant or on a tour.

* Do what the signs tell you to do in any place you visit, indoors or outdoors. Those signs are there to protect the things you have come to see and when you obey the signs you save those interesting things for some other girl to see.

* Protect all living things—animals, birds, and plants. Be a friend to animals by doing what the signs in the zoo say. Be a friend to wildlife by looking quietly. Let flowers grow by walking around the edges of gardens and using the paths.

* Leave gates and doors just as you found them, either open or closed. Fences protect animals and people and plants.

* Pick up after yourself as you travel. Throw wrappers and paper cups and what is left of your lunch in a trash basket. Leave no trace of your trip in the camp site or picnic area, in the bus or train, on the street. Leave every place you go ready for the next visitors.

60

After You Come Back

Talk about your trip at the next troop meeting. Tell your troop what you liked best. Listen to them tell what they will always remember.

Thank everyone who helped with your trip.

Think about how your next trip can be even better. What did you bring that you wished you had left at home? What equipment did you need that you didn't bring? What did you wish you knew how to do?

Where do you want to go next time?

CAMPING

When you go camping you do exciting things out-of-doors. You hike along green trails and you hunt for animal tracks or signs of the changing season. You swim and play outdoor games. You sing around a campfire with old friends and new ones.

Girl Scouts do three kinds of camping. They go for the day to day camp. They live for two weeks at a camp called an established camp. They go for two or three nights with their troop and that is called troop camping.

DAY CAMPING

You come from home every morning and you spend the day out-of-doors at your Girl Scout council's day camp. You camp with other Scouts from troops in your town. You bring your lunch from home and often cook it over a fire. When it rains you do rainy day things under shelter nearby. You and your new friends will be in troop-size groups called units. Each unit has a grownup leader. In the evening you go home to sleep. Perhaps one time while you are going to day camp, you will be able to stay and sleep there overnight.

ESTABLISHED CAMPING

At an established camp you live in camp. At night you sleep in a tent or a cabin. You make friends with girls who come from other troops. Your leaders are called counselors and they know new songs and games and things to do. You can work on different badges. You sing around a blazing campfire. You play wide games. You help put on a play in a woodland theatre. You improve your swimming.

TROOP CAMPING

You and your troop go camping at your Girl Scout council's camp or other places your council finds for you. You may go for a weekend, for two or three days during a vacation, or for a whole week. You can go in the spring, in the fall, in the summer, and maybe in the winter to a cabin.

You plan troop camping. Your troop has decided to go troop camping and now you make your plans.

First, when can you go? Your troop leader will find out for you when your troop can use the camp site and she will reserve it for you. She will also find out what equipment is there and whether you will sleep in a tent or a cabin.

Then, how will you get to the camp site? On a bus? By car? When you decide this, you can set the time for leaving to go to camp and the time you will get back from camp.

How will you pack your clothes and equipment and food so that you can carry it yourselves from the car or bus?

How much will it all cost? To find out the cost of your trip, add together the camp site fee and the transportation and food costs. Then decide whether the troop treasury will pay or whether each girl will pay for herself.

Once you know when you are going and how much it will cost, you can tell your parents all about the trip and ask for their permission to go.

What will you eat? You and your troop plan what you will eat at every meal. You can find menu ideas in the chapter, "Cooking and Eating." For the first meal at camp each girl could bring her own food. If there is no place to store foods that must be kept cold, plan to have food that does not need to be refrigerated. If you know what cooking equipment there will be at camp, it will help you plan. Are there fireplaces indoors, outdoors? Or will there be a stove—a quick cooking gas stove or a slow cooking wood stove? Once you have a shopping list of the food you need, you can figure out how much it will all cost.

Three ways to carry things

66

Make a List of Things To Do

There are so many things to do at camp. There are so many ways to use all the skills you have learned at troop meetings. You can learn to know the sky, the woods, the birds. You can use your knowledge of the compass and trail signs to play a wide game.

Make a list of what you want to do at camp and then write down what you need to know to do these things. Now you know what to plan and practice during your troop meetings. Your patrol can bring blankets to troop meetings and practice making a bedroll. Practice building fires and lashing. Plan your campfires and flag ceremonies. Practice at troop meetings will leave you more time to try out new things at camp.

Plan for religious services if you are going to be at camp on a Saturday or Sunday.

Kaper Charts for a Cabin Weekend

KAPERS BY BUDDIES

	COOKS	CLEANUP	WOOD FIRES WATER	TABLE SETTERS, SWEEPERS
FRIDAY NIGHT	MARY- BETTY	JANE- LYNN	KATHY- JOYCE	PEGGY- LINDA
SATURDAY MORNING	JUDY- CAROL	MARY- BETTY	JANE- LYNN	KATHY- JOYCE
SATURDAY NOON	PEGGY- LINDA	JUDY- CAROL	MARY- BETTY	JANE- LYNN
SUNDAY MORNING	KATHY- JOYCE	PEGGY- LINDA	JUDY- CAROL	MARY- BETTY
SUNDAY NOON	JANE- LYNN	KATHY- JOYCE	PEGGY- LINDA	JUDY- CAROL

KAPERS BY PATROLS

	COOKS AND CLEANUPS	WOOD, FIRES, WATER, FLAG	TABLE SETTERS, SWEEPERS
FRIDAY SUPPER	 (bird)	 (holly leaf)	 (flower)
SATURDAY BREAKFAST	 (flower)	 (bird)	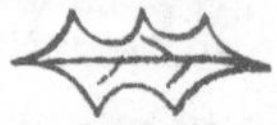 (holly leaf)
SATURDAY NOON	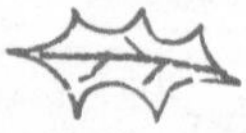 (holly leaf)	 (flower)	 (bird)

FINAL CLEANUP

SWEEP CABIN CLOSE SHUTTERS	
FILL WOODPILE CLEAN LANTERNS EMPTY WATER PAILS	
PACK FOOD CLEANUP KITCHEN	

COOK

CLEAN-UP

FIRE BUILDER

Make a kaper chart for jobs to be done at camp. List the jobs.
Then decide how the jobs will be divided up and how many
times a day each job needs to be done. Now make a kaper
chart to fit your plans. Remember to make a final cleanup
chart.

Equipment You Will Need

You can start to collect and make your own equipment even before you go camping. Then you will be ready for hikes and trips with your troop and outings with your family. Put your name on your own equipment. Always put your equipment away in one place ready to use on your next trip.

FOR YOURSELF

Knife

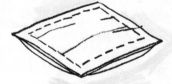

Rope—about 8 feet long

Bandana

Compass

Sit-upon—waterproof square big enough to sit on.

Cooking kit—plate, cup, fork, spoon, small frying pan and kettle, a bag to keep it all in.

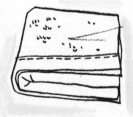

Ground cloth and bed-roll or sleeping bag.

Sack—to carry and store your equipment in.

Waterproof matches.

Pot holders.

FOR YOUR PATROL

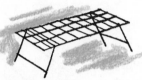

Grill or sturdy rack—
to hold pots over fire.

Frying pan, nest of ket-
tles or a large kettle,
can opener, big stirring
spoon, pancake turner.

First aid kit.

Water pail—to use as fire
bucket and to carry things.

Pack basket or tote
bag—to carry and
store patrol equipment.

KETTLES

You need: Tin cans of different sizes,
pieces of wire or wire clothes hangers,
punch can opener or nail and hammer.

1. Make two holes opposite each other
just under top of can. Use can opener or
hammer and nail to make holes.

2. Take a piece of wire and push each
end through a hole. Twist each end up
so that it will not slip out. Shape wire into
a handle.

Do this to each tin can. When you have
turned all the cans into kettles, store them
by putting the smallest kettle inside the
next size. Then you will have a nest of
kettles.

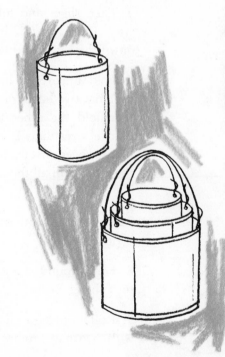

A BEDROLL

You need: Ground cloth, blankets, sleeping sheet, blanket pin, piece of rope.

1. Place poncho or waterproof ground cloth flat on ground. Ground cloth should be foot longer than blankets to protect them and to keep you dry.

2. Place first blanket down center of ground cloth.

3. Place second blanket down center of first blanket.

4. Add other blankets in the same way as the first and second blankets.

5. Take sheet and fold in half the long way. Place on top blanket with edges down the center of blanket.

6. Fold uncovered half of top blanket over the two edges of sleeping sheet and then fold the other half of next-to-top blanket over that. Continue folding each blanket over, first from one side then from the other. Pin all the blankets together at one end.

7. Pack some clothes and equipment in bedroll.

8. Fold ground cloth over blankets and tuck the ends in.

9. Roll from bottom to top and tie up with two half hitches (see page 102)

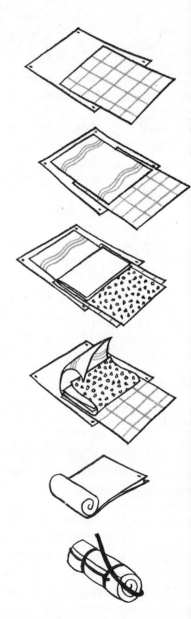

Living in a Tent

When you live in a tent you live a special way. You are closer to the woods and the stars and your friends—you may have three of them sleeping in the tent with you.

You do some things differently from the way you do them in your room at home. Everything must be put away at night because anything you leave out may be wet with dew in the morning. Put your clothes in plastic bags when you pack at home. Keep them in those bags at camp so they will stay dry at night. Plastic bags also help you keep your tent neat and make things easy to find.

Tent ropes are there to hold up your tent and nothing else! If you hang things on them, you will have a sagging tent. You will need a clothesline for just such things as wet clothes. You can put up a rope clothesline (see page 101) or you can lash a clothes rack (see page 103).

Pins make holes in tents and start tears that let the rain in, so never pin anything to a tent. Nails in tent poles split and weaken them. You can make a hook for your jacket by lashing a forked stick to your tent pole (see page 104).

A mirror can burn your canvas, because sunlight reflected in the mirror can make enough heat to burn. Protect your tent by putting your mirror under cover.

When it rains, do not touch the tent canvas. Touching it breaks the air bubbles in the cloth and that lets the rain through. Don't be the one to start a leak in your tent!

Once your tent canvas is wet, let it dry out in the sun and air. Make sure the sides and flaps are dry before you roll them up.

When You Go Camping

The air is clear or maybe it is damp. It does not matter. You are at camp! Where will you sleep and where will you eat? Where does that path lead?

You waste not a minute. Make up your bed and put your things away. Check the kaper chart to find your job. Maybe it will be opening shutters or gathering wood or unpacking food supplies or getting lanterns ready.

Camp life goes into full swing with every girl doing her share. It is almost supper time and cooks begin to get ready. "Hoppers"—girls who are going to serve—set the table. Other girls get the campfire ready or explore a trail.

Then you hear that welcome cry "Come and get it." Suddenly you find you have never been so hungry before. And everything tastes so good.

After supper you sing songs around a glowing campfire, one patrol acts out a song and another tells a legend.

Then—too soon—it is time to get washed and ready for bed. Your leader may read you a story while the wind whispers through the trees. You listen to the night sounds. Then you all settle down at the time you agreed upon so that everybody can be ready for the fun tomorrow.

Before you know it the birds are singing and you are up and ready to go. You do your breakfast kapers and then straighten your cabin or tent.

So much to see, so much to do! What did you plan at troop meeting — a lunch hike or cookout? Did you decide to work on a badge, lash a shelf, look for birds?

The day speeds by. Another supper, another campfire, another day of fun to remember.

The last day comes and you leave the camp site in good condition for the next group.

Your cabin or tent is spotless.
The woodpile is full.
The leftover food is packed to take home.
There are no paper scraps in sight.

It is time to go. When can you come back? Soon you hope.

FINDING THE WAY

A good traveler can find the way on the city sidewalks or on unmarked mountain trails. She knows where she is going and where she has been. She can tell another person how to find the way. She can help her troop and family on a trip.

You can find the way if you are alert so that you see the right signs and if you can read maps so that you know what to look for.

Keep your eyes open at all times. Notice street names and try to remember them. Test yourself to see whether you can name all the streets in your neighborhood and the places where the main streets cross. In the country, look for landmarks such as barns, crossroads, signs, filling stations. In the woods, watch for special trees or ponds or big rocks or trail signs.

Maps Help You Find the Way

City maps tell you where all the streets are and also railroad stations and museums and monuments. They make exploring a town more fun.

During a troop meeting use a street map. Find your meeting place on the map and chart a hike from your meeting place to some place in your neighborhood and back. Then go out and find the streets that you picked for your hike.

Road maps tell you how to get some place by car. Road maps tell you whether roads are main roads or back roads, whether there is another—or alternate—way to get to the same place. Look at a road map—your parents may have one you can use or your patrol can ask for one at a neighborhood filling station.

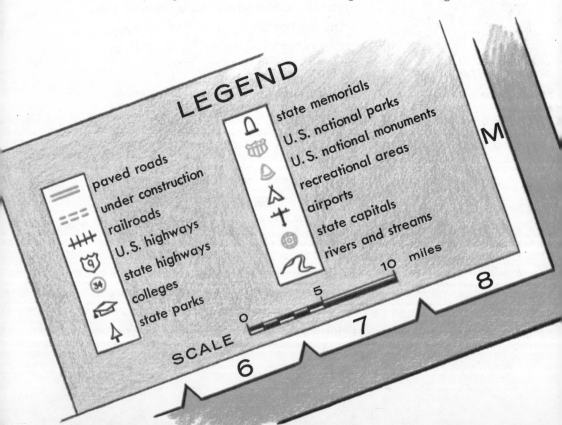

LEGEND

paved roads
under construction
railroads
U.S. highways
state highways
colleges
state parks

state memorials
U.S. national parks
U.S. national monuments
recreational areas
airports
state capitals
rivers and streams

SCALE

0   5   10   miles

M

6   7   8

At the corner of the map you will find a box called a legend. The legend explains what the marks on the map mean. You must read the legend and understand it if you are going to use a road map correctly.

Look for these things in the legend: Signs that explain the types of roads, a sign for railroad tracks or for a bridge, the date the map was made and who made it.

Old maps in a museum tell you how a city used to be or how explorers thought your state was, where the rivers went and where there were forests. It is fun to compare an old map with an up-to-date map.

Sketch Maps

You, yourself, can make a map for other people to follow. You can make a sketch map.

A sketch map is one you draw to show someone how to get to a certain place. You put on your sketch map just what a person needs to know to get to that spot. If you are making a map of a place in town, show the streets the person will walk along, where he will turn, landmarks that will keep him from getting lost. Landmarks might be a firehouse, a church, a grocery store, a vacant lot, a school.

Do you know how long it takes to get from one place to another? Put that in. When you tell someone it takes about ten minutes to walk from the library to Grove Street, you give him an idea of the distance.

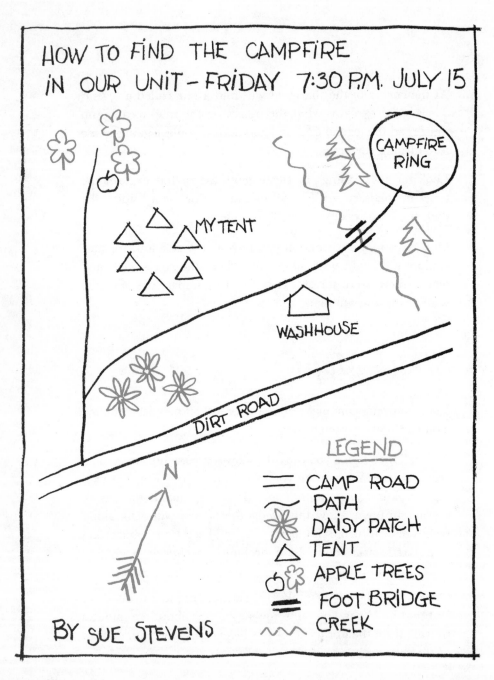

You may not have room to write in all the words you need, so make a legend and put that on a blank corner of your map. In the legend explain what you mean by each mark you have used. If you are using traffic lights as landmarks, make up a sign that means traffic light. Use the sign on the map and put the explanation in the legend. Have a sign for fence, road, and path. Be sure to include your name, the date, and the title of the map.

You can use sketch maps at troop meetings and at camp. You can trade maps with other girls or another patrol to see whether they can follow your map.

Now draw a sketch map that will:

* Show a friend how to get from her house to your house.

* Direct a Girl Scout from another troop to your meeting place.

* Invite someone to a party and mark the spot for it.

* Guide your patrol on a treasure hunt.

* Record the interesting things you saw on a hike.

* Show your parents what your camp site is like.

* Tell a new girl how to find the library, the post office, the grocery store.

Keep going

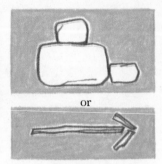

Go this way

or

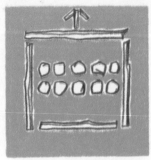

Go ten steps this way

Split your group
half go left, half go right

Camp is this way

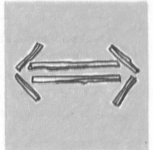

Turn around and
go back

Trail Signs

There is a split in the trail. Which way to go? You know in a flash by the rocks in a row!

When you want to tell another patrol which way to go in the woods or fields you can leave a message for that person. You can use sticks or stones or yarn or tags to tell them where to go next.

Stone or stick messages are easy to make and will not blow away.

Tags or pieces of yarn make good trail markers. Tie the yarn or tags to trees, to bunches of grass, to rocks. Place each trail

82

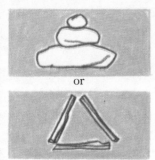
or

fork
in
path

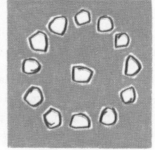
fork
in
path

Danger

Stop—go the other way

Wait here for next direction

End of the trail
"I have gone home."

Trail signs may be made out of rocks or stones or little pebbles. They can be drawn in dirt or sand. Use what you find.

marker within sight of the next one. The last person on the trail collects all the markers.

Notes. You can lay a trail with notes. A note might say, "Follow the creek till you come to the fallen tree. Look in the hollow end of the tree." The note found in the hollow end of the tree tells where to go next.

Compass directions. Instead of saying go left or right or straight ahead, you can use compass directions to lay a trail. Of course you have to learn how to give compass directions first (see page 84). You can make up a wide game (see page 162) using compass directions.

Using a Compass

A compass needle is really a small magnet. Like all magnets, the tip of the needle—colored red or blue or black or marked with an N—turns toward the magnetic north of the earth. But that tip also moves toward iron or steel. If you have your jackknife close to your compass, this tip will move toward the knife and not toward the north.

The letters on your compass are N for north, E for east, S for south, and W for west. To orient your compass, hold it flat in your hand and turn it until the N on the compass is under that "north pointing" tip of the needle. (On some compasses, the needle cannot swing freely until the stem is unwound.)

Now you know where north is. By looking at the compass you can see where east is, and south and west. If you want to go directly south, you go toward S. But maybe you want to go somewhere between east and south. The points between E and S are ESE, SE, SSE. Learn all the points on the compass, starting at N and going toward E all the way around to N again. This is called "boxing the compass."

Then there are numbers on a compass. They are called degrees and there are 360 of them. The sign for degree is ° and when you read "120°" you say "120 degrees." (North is both 0° and 360°.) You could be directed to go N or to go 360°, and it would mean the same thing.

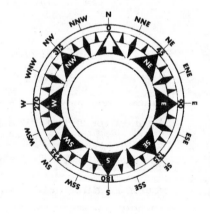

compass card

84

To follow compass directions do this. Your directions say "go east" so you:

1. Hold the compass flat so that E is in front of you.

2. Orient the compass by turning *yourself* around in a circle—still holding your compass so that E is in front of you—until the needle points to N.

3. Now you face E. Walk straight ahead and you will be going east.

To give compass directions. If you are laying a trail and you want to find a compass direction you do this.

1. Face the landmark you are taking the direction of—say a tree—holding your compass in front of you.

2. Orient the compass by turning *it* around so that the needle points to N.

3. Now you have found the direction of the tree. Look at your compass. What point on the compass is facing the tree? Suppose it is 300°. You put on your map "go 300°."

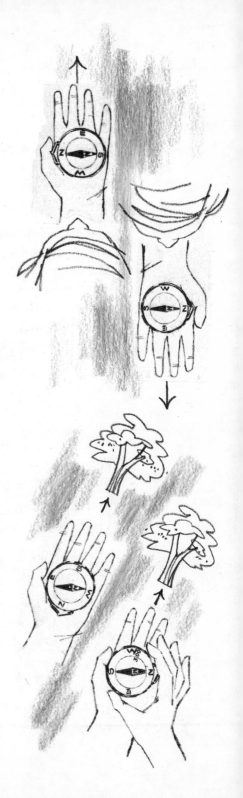

When you give directions be sure to include the exact spot where you stood when you took the compass reading. If you were standing on a flat rock, say, "Start at the flat rock and go 90°."

You may use a Silva compass. This compass has an "orienting arrow" on the face to help you get the compass in position. The outside of the compass is a metal ring called a "housing case." You can turn the housing case around on the plastic base and move the orienting arrow. When the arrow is under the needle, the compass is oriented.

On the base there is also an arrow—marked "Direction of Travel." This arrow will tell you which way to go.

Following directions with a Silva compass. Suppose you are told to go 120°:

1. Turn the housing case around until 120° is at the Direction of Travel arrow.

2. Hold compass so Direction of Travel arrow points straight ahead of you.

3. Orient the compass: Turn *yourself* around in a circle until the orienting arrow on the face is right under the needle, pointing the same way.

4. Now you are oriented and you face 120°. Walk straight ahead and you will be going 120°.

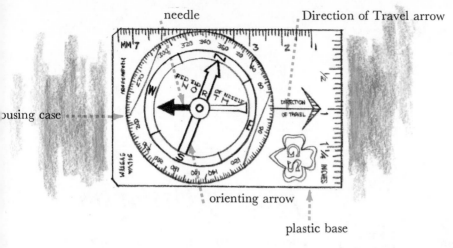

needle   Direction of Travel arrow

housing case

orienting arrow

plastic base

Giving directions with a Silva compass.
If you want to give a compass direction
you do this:

1. Face the thing you want to get the
compass direction of—a gate perhaps.

2. Hold the plastic base so that the Direction of Travel arrow points toward the
gate.

3. Orient the compass: Turn the housing
case around until the orienting arrow is
right under the needle and points the
same way.

4. Now you have found the direction of
the gate. Look at the number at the beginning of the Direction of Travel arrow.

That number is the direction you give.
If it is 90°, you say "Go 90° from this spot."

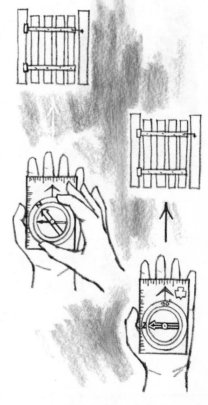

87

Judging Distances

There will be times when you will need to know a distance or a measurement and you will not have a ruler with you. Then you can use your own special ruler to judge by. You can use yourself.

Your own personal measurements can help you measure how high something is, how wide it is, or how far away.

Length is something you can measure with your own feet. How long is your right foot? Measure it. Suppose it measures 8 inches. Walk off the length you want to measure—say a rug. Walk the rug by placing one foot in front of the other, heel touching toe. How many steps did you take? Suppose you took 10 steps and each step was 8 inches, multiply 10 by 8 and you get 80 inches. That is the length or distance. When you have a large number of inches, it is better to convert inches to feet and have a smaller number. One foot on a ruler equals 12 inches. So divide 12 inches into 80 inches. The rug is 6 feet 8 inches long.

Your pace. You can use your own pace to measure longer distances. Measure off a ten-foot distance. Then walk off the ten feet and count your steps. Do this until you are sure you have the number of steps right. Now you know how many steps it takes you to go ten feet. If you get instructions to "walk ten feet and turn right" you will know how many paces to go. Do the same thing for twenty feet or fifty feet.

What are some distances it would be handy to pace off? When you take a picture, how far from your subject should you stand? Six feet? Measure off six feet and then pace it. The next time you take a picture, pace off the distance.

Scout's pace. Scout's pace is walking a certain number of paces, then jog trotting the same number. Walk twenty, jog trot twenty. Scout's pace is a good way to measure distance and time. It is a good way to travel distances quickly without getting tired.

Time. Find out how long it takes you to walk a mile comfortably. Then when someone tells you a place is a mile away you will know how long it takes to get there.

Width. You can tell how wide or long something is by measuring against yourself. Put your arm out straight and hold a ruler against your arm with one end at your finger tips. Where does 12 inches (one foot) come to? Where does 3 feet (one yard) come to? Hold out both arms and ask a friend to measure you. When you know how to judge a yard, you can tell whether you have 6 feet of rope or only 3 feet.

Find one of your finger joints that measures one inch. Use this measure when you look for a stick an inch thick.

Height. You can use a pencil to measure a tree. First ask a friend whose height you know to stand against the tree. You stand far away. Hold a pencil straight up in your fist, with your arm out straight in front of you. Close one eye. With your thumb, mark off the height of your friend on the pencil. Then see how many times this pencil height goes up the tree. Suppose it goes up the tree 5 times. Your friend is 50 inches high. Multiply her height by 5: 50 inches x 5 = 250 inches. Change 250 inches into feet by dividing it by 12. The tree is over 20 feet high.

Weight. Learn to judge weight by the feel. First hold something that weighs a pound—say a one pound box of sugar. Hold it until you count to five. Put it down. Pick it up again and hold it for five counts again. Do this with the other hand. Now pick up a book. Does it weigh more or less? Check the weight on a scale. Next hold objects that weigh half a pound —say a full eight-ounce can. Try something that weighs five pounds—flour or a bag of potatoes. Then test yourself by lifting an unmarked object. Keep testing and checking yourself until you are sure you know what each weight feels like.

JUDGING CONTEST

You need: Measuring sticks or tapes and a list of things to be measured—length of room or tent, distance between two points, height of door or tree, weight of package.

1. Find your personal measurements and write them down. To get them, either work with another girl—you can measure each other—or set up measuring stations where each girl has her foot, height, and hand spread measured.

2. Use your measurements to judge the measurements of the things on the list. Write down your guesses.

3. When everyone has finished, the game leader announces the correct answers. How good a judge are you?

MY PERSONAL MEASUREMENTS

My height is _____

My foot length is _____

My hand spread from thumb to little finger is _____

My arm spread from hand to hand is _____

The height I can reach is _____

My _____ finger joint is one inch.

My pace is _____

It takes me _____ to walk a mile.

KNOTS AND LASHING

A Girl Scout uses knots and lashing in so many ways. She uses a square knot to fasten her Girl Scout tie. She uses a bowline knot to make a loop so she can pull someone to safety. She lashes sticks together to make a table.

Learn these knots and ways of lashing and then practice them every chance you get. Bring your rope to troop meetings and play games using these knots. At camp, practice while you wait for lunch. Make them blindfolded.

Be prepared to make them in a hurry!

Finishing off Your Rope

If the ends of your rope are not held together in some way, they will unravel. To stop that from happening you can do one of three things:

Knot the ends. Knot the ends of the rope by making an overhand knot. This "stopper" knot will keep the rope from slipping through a hole. It is not good for rope used for knot tying.

Tape the ends. This method is quick and easy but good for only a short time because the tape will loosen and come off.

Whip the ends. This is the best way to finish off rope. You should finish off your knot-tying rope this way.

93

WHIPPING A ROPE

You need: A piece of rope and a piece of string or cord 12 inches long. Use brightly colored string to decorate your jump rope or ropes on a drawstring bag.

1. Make a loop with one end of the string and lay the loop along the rope with the ends of the string hanging off the end of the rope.

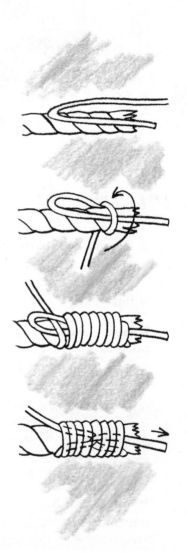

2. Hold the string in place with your left thumb. With your right hand, wind the long end of the string tightly over the loop and around the rope. The short end will be left hanging.

3. Wind the string around the rope for at least an inch. Wind firmly and closely but do not overlap. When you have wound far enough, tuck end you have been winding through loop. Hold it with your left hand thumb so it does not loosen.

4. Take the other end and pull slowly. The loop will disappear under the winding. Pull until the loop is halfway under the winding. Trim the ends to make a neat finish.

If your whipping slips off the rope, you did not make it tight enough. Practice until it holds when you try to push it off.

94

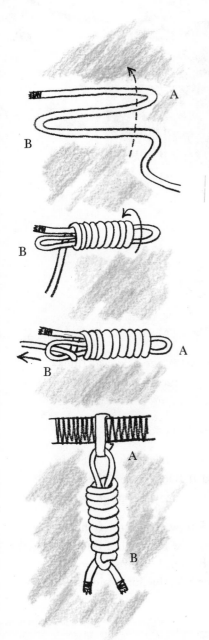

HANKING A ROPE

Use it: To carry a rope on your belt; to store a rope.

1. Fold one end of rope in two loops about six or seven inches long. Size of loops depend on length of rope.

2. Wrap long end of rope evenly around the loops, starting at A and working toward B.

3. When you get to B, stick the end of the rope you have been wrapping through the loop.

4. Pull one side of A gently to see which will tighten B and anchor the end of the rope. Then pull loop tight.

5. The two ends of the rope will be uneven. Make them even by pulling gently on A or on one of the ends.

6. Roll hank between your palms to smooth it.

7. Hang it on your belt.

Unwind it by pulling the end that did not go through the loop. Pull it all the way through the wound rope.

Knots and Hitches

SQUARE KNOT

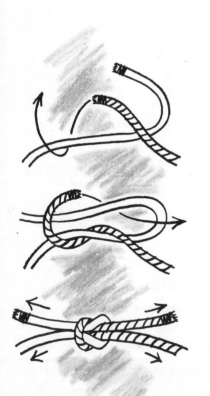

Use it: To join two ropes of equal thickness; tie a package; mend a broken rope or shoelace; tie a bandage for first aid.

1. Take a rope end in each hand.

2. Cross the right hand end over the left hand rope. Bend it back under, then forward and up. The ends will change hands.

3. Cross the end now in your left hand over, back, under and forward of the end now in your right hand. The short ends should lie flat beside the long pieces of rope.

4. Pull tight.

Untie a square knot by holding the ropes on both sides of the knot and pushing them toward the center. Or take one end and yank it hard toward the center of the knot. Then you can slip the rope ends apart.

Many Girl Scouts say this as they tie this knot:

Right over left and left over right
Makes the knot neat and tidy and tight!

MAGICIAN'S TRICK

You need: Three colored handkerchiefs and a tube.

1. Tie the handkerchiefs together using square knots. Do not pull the knots tight.

2. Push them into the tube, yanking the knots as you do. Do this by pulling hard on one end of the knot. Practice this until you can do it smoothly.

3. Pull the handkerchiefs from the opposite end, slipping them apart as you pull them out.

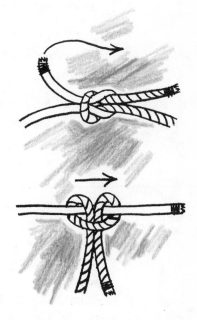

SHEET BEND

Sailors call some of the ropes used on sails, "sheets." A "bend" is a way of making a loop.

Use it: To tie together big ropes and little ropes—a square knot works only when two ropes are the same thickness.

1. Take the little rope or cord in your right hand and the big rope in your left hand. Tie a square knot but do not pull it tight. If you want to experiment, pull it tight and see what happens. Then tie another square knot.

2. Cross the short end of the cord *over* the long part of the cord and stick the end of it down into loop of the rope.

3. Pull long end of cord and long end of rope to tighten.

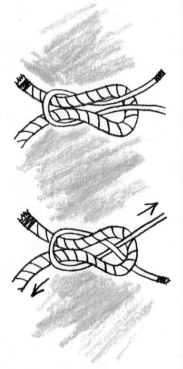

A Girl Scout watched two men trying to hang a big, heavy curtain for a stage play. The men tried to tie two ropes together but one was much larger than the other and every knot was pulled apart by the weight of the curtain. The men were ready to say, "It can't be done." Then the Girl Scout offered to help. The men looked at her surprised. If they could not do it how could she? But they said, "Go ahead." She tied a sheet bend and it held fast!

CLOVE HITCH

Use it: To fasten one end of a rope around a post or tree; to put up a clothesline or badminton net; to start lashing. Do not use it to hold a moving object, such as an animal, because the moving will loosen the hitch.

1. Take one end of rope in your right hand. With left hand hold rest of rope across front of post.

2. Pass end of rope around in back of post.

3. Bring it around to front of post. Cross it over long part, making an X. Hold X with left thumb and forefinger.

4. Pass rope to the right again, wrapping it around post *below* first turn.

5. Push rope end under X, going from left to right so that it comes out between the two turns around post.

6. Pull short end to the right, long end to the left. As long as there is a steady pull on the long end the hitch will not loosen.

Practice tying the knot to the left. Then try tying it up and down on a cross-bar.

Untie or loosen it by pushing both ends toward the center.

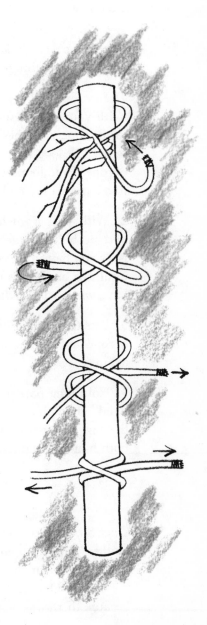

BOWLINE

Use it: To make a loop that will not slip
—for hanging things or for lifesaving.

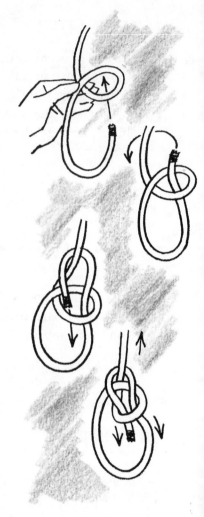

1. Lay long end of rope in your left hand.
With your right hand make a little loop
in the rope just where you want the knot
to be. The loop must go *over* the long part
of rope. Hold loop in place with your left
hand and let the end hang down in front.

2. With your right hand take short end
and push it up through the little loop.
Now you have another loop. Pull the end
until this big loop is the size you want to
have when you are finished.

3. Pass this end around behind long part
of rope and then down through little loop
again.

4. Hold long part of rope with your left
hand. Hold short end and right side of
the big loop with your right. Pull with
both hands to tighten.

Once a boat was swept over Niagara Falls. In it were a father,
mother, and son. People standing on a bridge over the Falls
saw the accident. A man quickly threw a rope to the three in
the water. One caught it but it slipped through his hands
because there was neither a loop nor a knot to hold on to.

100

CLOTHESLINE WITHOUT CLOTHESPINS

You need: Two or three ropes, one longer than the others.

1. Lay ropes together as in picture.

2. Hold the ropes as if they were one rope and tie one end together with an overhand knot.

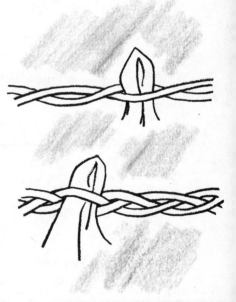

3. Now braid the ropes if you have three ropes. Twist them if you have two.

4. Finish with an overhand knot.

5. Attach clothesline to trees or posts with clove hitches or bowlines.

6. Hang things on the line by catching them between the twisted or braided ropes.

101

TWO HALF HITCHES

Use this: To fasten the end of a rope after it has been looped over a post, around a bedroll, through a ring, around a flagpole.

1. Loop the end of the rope around the post or through the ring.

2. Take the short end of the rope and wrap it under and over the long part of the rope, pushing the end down through the loop. *This is a half hitch.*

3. Make a second half hitch on the long rope below the first half hitch and you will have two half hitches.

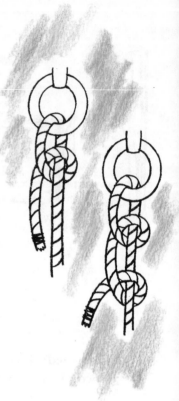

Lashing

You can make outdoor shelves and racks, flagpoles and hooks, all without using nails. You lash them in place.

Lashing is a method of fastening sticks and poles together using binder twine or cord or string. Practice lashing at troop meetings so that when you go camping you will be prepared to lash quickly and correctly.

Before you can start lashing, you must know how to tie a clove hitch, a half hitch, and a square knot.

You need sticks and twine to practice with. If you cannot cut sticks from trees, you can use broomsticks, dowel sticks, bamboo poles.

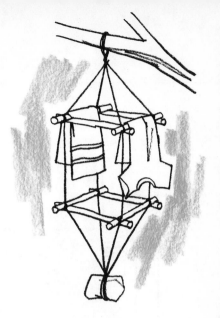

SQUARE LASHING

Use it: To make racks for towels or bathing suits, coat hangers, picture frames.

You need: Two sticks and a long piece of cord.

1. Tie a clove hitch to upright stick. Be sure knot is on side of stick and long end of cord is in front of you. Place other stick across upright stick.

2. Pass long end of cord down over cross stick and around in back of upright stick. Bring cord to front under cross stick. Then bring up and over cross stick and in back of upright. Bring down over cross stick as in beginning.

3. Wind exactly this way about three times. Pull cord tightly as you work to make it lie neatly beside earlier turns.

4. Now you are ready for "frapping." Wind the cord about three times *between* the two sticks to tighten. Pull as tight as you can.

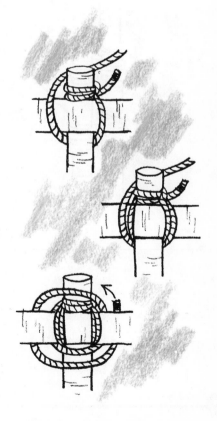

5. To finish, make two half hitches around one stick. Or tie the two ends together with a square knot. Trim the ends and tuck them underneath the lashing.

103

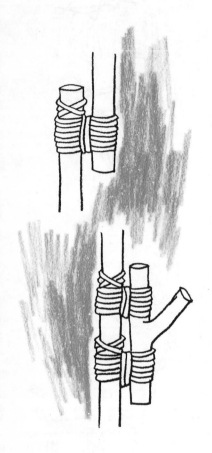

SHEER OR ROUND LASHING

Use it: To extend a pole; to make a hook; to mend a broken table or chair leg.

1. Make a clove hitch around one stick.

2. Place the bottom of the second stick against the top of the first stick.

3. Wind the cord around both sticks until they stay in position.

4. Frap three times to tighten. Finish with two half hitches or tie ends with a square knot. Tuck ends under.

CONTINUOUS LASHING

Use it: To make a table top or shelf.

You need: Two long poles which you have square lashed to legs; cross sticks wide enough to go across the two poles with an inch left over on each side (number of cross sticks will depend on how long table is); two pieces of cord, each one four times the length of the table top.

Three girls make a good team for continuous lashing.

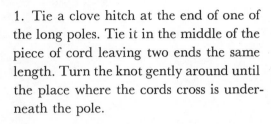

First girl 1. Tie a clove hitch at the end of one of the long poles. Tie it in the middle of the piece of cord leaving two ends the same length. Turn the knot gently around until the place where the cords cross is underneath the pole.

2. Roll cords into two balls so they will not get tangled as you use them.

Second girl Do steps 1 and 2 on the other pole tying the clove hitch directly opposite the first hitch.

Third girl 3. Lay cross sticks in place.

First and second girl 4. Each take a ball of cord in each hand. Pull the cords toward you up and over the cross stick.

5. Pull the cords under the long pole and cross them making an X with the cords on the under side of the pole.

6. Lay the next stick in place and repeat steps 4 and 5. Continue until table top or shelf is finished.

7. Finish off with a square knot. Tuck the ends under.

To make your table top sturdier, notch the long pole and the cross sticks so they fit into each other.

YOUR KNIFE

You can carry your pocketknife with you whenever you go Scouting—at troop meetings or at camp, inside or outside, because the blade folds back neatly into its handle.

Before you use your knife—before you even open it—check to see that you have enough room. Swing your arms in a half circle in front of you and then to the side. If you do not touch yourself or another person or any object, you have enough room. You have an "arc of safety."

Using Your Knife

Open and close your knife with *both* hands. Then your fingers will be behind the blade if it snaps closed.

Close your knife when you finish using it so another person will not step or fall or sit on an open blade. Close your knife when you walk around so that if you trip you will not cut yourself or someone else.

Grasp the handle of your knife firmly. Push with your whole hand.

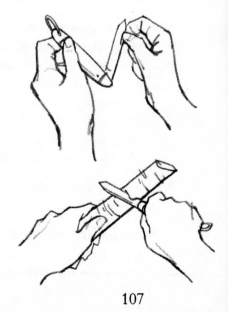

To make a point. Cut toward the end of the stick, digging the blade in as you go down the stick. Turn the stick as you cut to make an even point.

To trim a branch. Start at the thick end of the branch and work toward the top. You can get a better grip when you hold the stronger end and cut the weaker. This way you will not split the stick.

To cut green sticks. Always cut from a place where there are many sticks so the one you use will not be missed. Look for a stick that has the shape you need. Cut close to the ground. Cut on a slant, not straight across. If the stick is thick, cut from two sides to make a V. Leave a smooth edge not a jagged cut.

To cut vegetables. Cut down on a cutting board.

To whittle. Have a sharp knife and take small cuts. You can whittle a toggle from a twig and use it as a button for a belt.

108

Keep Your Knife Ready To Use

Clean it. Wipe the blade after you use it so it will not become rusty or sticky. Remove rust with steel wool. Keep the joints oiled so they do not become stiff.

Keep it sharp. If your knife is sharp it will dig into the stick you are cutting. A dull knife is more dangerous and more difficult to use than a sharp one.

To sharpen your knife use a kitchen sharpener or a sharpening stone called a carborundum. Lay the blade on the surface. Move it in a circle. Turn the blade over and sharpen the other side. Keep your fingers below the surface of the stone.

Use your knife only to cut wood, vegetables, rope, soap.

You may nick the blade when you use it on hard objects and if you stick it into the ground or use it to pry something open you may break it. You may break the handle if you use it as a hammer.

Using a Saw

Use a saw to cut wood that is too thick for your knife. Saw with a push-pull motion. Do not push too hard because if you do, the blade will get caught in the wood and will bend. To saw a log, use a sawhorse to hold the log in place. A bow saw is good for cutting logs.

FIRES

Before you can cook outdoors you must have a fire. Your fire may be very small, just big enough to cook a pancake, or it may be large enough to cook food for your whole patrol. Large or small, making the fire is half the fun of cooking.

Building a fire is a responsibility, too. You are older now and you can be trusted with fires. You can be trusted to do two things—to build a fire only where you have permission and to have a grownup around when you are building it.

Your troop may build fires in a park or camp site, in a member's backyard, on a gravel driveway or a beach. You can build a fire in a wheel barrow filled with dirt or in a sandbox. When you build a fire in any place, you are on your honor to get permission from the owner of a site. When you cook on a very small wood fire, work in three's so one girl can tend the fire while the second one cooks and the third eats.

Here are some ways Girl Scouts cook—a wood fire with a grill over it, a charcoal fire in a charcoal stove, and a Buddy burner fire in a vagabond stove.

Wood Fires

There are five steps to building a wood fire. They are:

1. Make a safe and suitable place.

2. Have a supply of tinder, kindling, and fuel.

3. Build a foundation fire.

4. Build it into the kind of fire you need.

5. Put out the fire as soon as you are through using it.

1. MAKE A SAFE AND SUITABLE PLACE

Pick out a good place for your fire and make it safe so the fire cannot spread or burn any thing or any person. Choose a spot where there are no overhanging tree boughs. Next clear the ground so the fire cannot possibly spread. Clear away anything that can burn—leaves, grass, sticks.

Now your spot is ready and you make a fireplace to support your grill, kettle, or frying pan. Make it out of logs or bricks or flat stones. Be sure not to pick slate, shale, or schist stones because these rocks break and sometimes explode when they get very hot. Find out whether there are rocks like these near where you live.

Another thing you need to make the place safe and suitable is something to put out the fire with—a bucket of water or sand or dirt and a shovel.

112

2. HAVE ON HAND A SUPPLY OF TINDER, KINDLING, AND FUEL

Your wood fire needs three different kinds of fire material—tinder, kindling, and fuel. The match lights the tinder, the tinder lights the kindling, and the kindling starts the fuel burning.

Tinder should start to burn as soon as it is touched with a lighted match and so it must be as thin as a match. Good tinder snaps as you break it. It does not crumble or bend. Use thin twigs, tops of dried weeds, wood shavings.

Kindling is little sticks and can be as small as a pencil or as thick as your thumb. Kindling should also snap, rather than crumble or bend.

Fuel is the larger wood that keeps your fire going. This wood should be seasoned wood—that is, cut many months ago and it should be dry.

Make a woodpile. Stack your wood in three separate piles—one for tinder, one for kindling, and one for fuel. Build your woodpile far enough from the fire that no sparks can fly into it no matter how the wind shifts. If you are camping over night, cover the woodpile with a piece of plastic or waterproof material to keep the wood dry during the night.

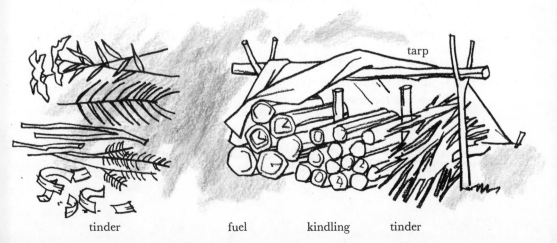

tinder   fuel   kindling   tinder

3. BUILD A FOUNDATION FIRE

This is a fire made with tinder and kindling and its job is to make enough heat to get the fuel burning.

Get your tinder and kindling ready. You need four handfuls of tinder and four handfuls of kindling. Make a rack with several pieces of kindling. Put the tinder on this rack instead of on the ground because this way the tinder has air underneath it and there is space for your match. Why air? Because in order to burn, a fire needs three elements—fuel, heat, and air. If you remember the fuel and the heat but forget air under your fuel your fire will not burn.

Next light the match. Kneel near the fire and strike the match away from your body. Tip the match down so that the flame catches on the matchstick. On a windy day, kneel with your back to the wind and cup your hands around the match.

Now light the tinder. Put the flame of the match under the tinder. Gently pile on more tinder. If necessary, blow at the base of the fire.

Add the kindling. When small tinder fire is going well, add kindling. Start with small pieces and gradually add bigger ones. Keep kindling close together but allow space for air.

4. BUILD IT INTO THE KIND OF FIRE YOU NEED

Tepee fire. This is a good fire for quick cooking since the heat is concentrated at one spot, the top. It looks like an Indian tepee and you use it under a kettle to boil water or to make stew. To make it, stack the fuel over the foundation fire. The foundation fire will start the fuel burning. Add fuel as you need it.

Crisscross fire. This kind of fire burns for a long time and makes good coals. It is good for broiling or toasting. It is good for a campfire. To make it, lay the fuel over the foundation fire in a crisscross pattern. Be sure to leave room for air. Add fuel as you need it.

Try not to put more wood on the fire than you need. A Girl Scout is thrifty. She uses as little wood as she can because it is one of her country's natural resources. She protects those resources.

Never leave a fire without a fire watcher. Agree among yourselves who is to watch the fire.

tepee fire   crisscross fire

5. PUT OUT THE FIRE AS SOON AS YOU ARE THROUGH USING IT

A fire is out when you can press your hand on the spot where it was and the ground around it. Sprinkle water all over the wood and ashes. Stir with a stick and sprinkle again until there are no live—burning—coals anywhere. If you do not have water, stir in sand or dirt until the fire is completely out. "Almost out" will not do!

FIREPLACE FIRES

Building a fire in a fireplace is like building a fire on the ground.

To make a fireplace "safe and suitable" you use a fire screen.

Your fire will need tinder, kindling, and logs. Three logs make the best fire. Be sure the logs touch each other at some point. Do not forget to leave space for air.

You build a foundation fire by making a tepee of kindling and leaning the tepee against the big logs. Or you can make a crisscross fire. Keep the ashes at the bottom of the fireplace to conserve heat.

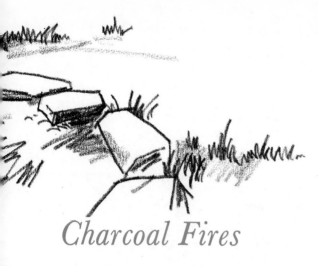

Charcoal Fires

Charcoal is a good fuel to use in back-
yards, driveways, parks, or places where
wood is scarce. In some places only charcoal fires are allowed. A charcoal fire
burns for a long time and needs little
refueling.

Start a charcoal fire half an hour before
you are ready to cook. Then the coals will
be hot enough to use. You need plenty
of tinder to get your charcoal fire
started. Do not use chemicals or liquid
starters because they are dangerous and
hard to handle. Charcoal needs air to
burn well, just as wood does, so raise it
off the ground. Use a grate to do this. You
will find instructions for building a charcoal fire on the next page.

When you finish cooking, put out the fire
with water. When the charcoal dries you
can keep it and use it again.

You can make a charcoal stove out of a
tin can.

117

CHARCOAL STOVE

You need: Tin can—No. 10 or larger, roll-type can opener, punch opener, wire for handle, three pieces sturdy wire screen.

1. Remove top of can with roll-type can opener. Punch airholes with punch opener around top and bottom of can.

2. Stick ends of wire through two of holes at top and twist to make a handle.

3. Push wire screen half way down into can to make a grate. This holds charcoal near the top for cooking and keeps air under charcoal. To keep screen from slipping, curl second piece of screen into a coil, and put between grate screen and bottom of stove.

4. Make a stove top out of the third piece of wire screen. This supports your hamburger or your pot.

To use a charcoal stove

Set the stove on cleared ground and put tinder on the grate. When tinder is burning briskly, drop charcoal into fire. Swing the stove by the handle now and then to keep the charcoal burning.

118

VAGABOND STOVE

You need: No. 10 tin can, pair of tin snips, gloves, roll-type can opener, punch opener, hammer.

1. Remove lid from tin can using roll-type can opener. This open end will be the bottom of your stove.

2. Cut a door in stove. Wearing gloves, take tin snips and cut from the open end two slits three inches apart and three inches long. Bend this piece of tin back into can and hammer it flat.

3. Punch with the punch opener two or three small holes at the top of the can on the side opposite the door. These are your air holes and serve as a chimney.

To use a vagabond stove

Find a level spot for the stove so food will not run over the side. If stove is not level, put a twig under the low edge.

Press the stove in the dirt so that it makes a ring. Then put it aside. Make a small fire of twigs in the ring. Keep fire small but steady. You can also use a Buddy burner.

Put the stove over the twig fire or Buddy burner. The stove will get very hot so do not touch it.

The first time you use your stove you will have to wipe the finish off the tin can after the stove has heated up. Hold stove with a pot holder and wipe off with a paper towel.

119

BUDDY BURNER

A Buddy burner is fuel and can be used with a vagabond stove. It is also good emergency fuel to have on hand if your stove at home should not work. You can use it in a driveway or an inside fireplace or when you cannot have an open fire. The smoke is very black so do not use it in a room.

You need: A shallow tin can; a strip of corrugated cardboard, a little narrower than the depth of the can; paraffin in a tin can; lid from a larger can; pot of water on the stove.

1. Roll cardboard into a coil that fits loosely into the can.

2. Melt the paraffin. Paraffin should always be melted in a tin can set in a pot of water on the stove. Use low heat. Melt small amounts at a time. The vapor given off by the melting paraffin might start to burn, so have a lid from a larger tin can on hand to smother any fire.

3. Fill shallow can almost to the top with the melted paraffin.

4. Let the paraffin harden. Now you have a Buddy burner.

You can make a Buddy burner using sawdust instead of cardboard. Fill the tin can with sawdust and pour in the paraffin.

To use a Buddy burner

Light the top of the Buddy burner with a match. Now you can cook on your vagabond stove. Never cook directly over a Buddy burner because the smoke is black and sooty.

Place the vagabond stove over the Buddy burner.

To put the fire out, turn the vagabond stove upside down on top of the Buddy burner and smother the flames. Use pot holders or a stick to lift and turn the stove. The paraffin will be hot and liquid, so wait until it cools and hardens before you pick up the Buddy burner.

WATERPROOF MATCHES

Waterproof your matches by dipping them into thin nail polish. You can dip them one at a time or in small bunches. Keep them in a small tin box along with a strip of sandpaper to strike them on.

Campfires

There is more to a fire than cooking. A fire can be magic too.

Day is done. Gone the sun. The fire crackles cozily and you and your friends sit around the campfire watching the magic of its flames. It may be a troop meeting at the end of a school day. It may be the end of a day at camp. There is nothing like a campfire!

It is a time for singing and music, for putting on skits and plays, for telling stories and reading poems. It is a time for going over the busy day's happenings and for making tomorrow's plans. It is a time for playing games, for toasting marshmallows. It is a time for sharing thoughts and dreams with good friends.

COOKING AND EATING

Eating is fun and so is fixing food to eat. Girl Scouts do both.

There are so many times and places to cook and eat.

At troop meetings—at your meeting place, on a hike, or a trip to the park—you can bring something from home and eat it. If there is some place to cook, you can grill a hamburger, toast a sandwich, fry eggs or french toast, cook pancakes. You can cook on a vagabond stove in someone's yard or driveway if you have permission. You can cook in a park or at a camp site.

Sometimes you will want to cook in a kitchen. Then you will go with your patrol to someone's house. Your troop leader will

arrange for this. Maybe you will be making refreshments for a troop party—cookies and cake. Maybe you will be doing part of a cooking badge.

At home you can make snacks after school. You can fix part of a meal and then prepare a whole meal. Learn to prepare breakfast and lunch and supper for your family so you can do it when your mother is away.

Experiment with new foods. Try to make something new, maybe a recipe from *American Girl* magazine. Sample new foods to see how they taste.

Make cooking and eating an adventure!

Food To Travel

Girl Scouts call lunches they carry in a bag "nosebags." The name comes from the bag of food that is hung under a horse's nose when he is away from his stable at mealtime.

When you pack your nosebag, put the heaviest things at the bottom and the light, crushable foods on top. Pack two napkins so you will have one for a tablecloth. Wrap each sandwich separately in waxed paper or aluminum foil. Pack the sandwiches standing on end so they will not get soggy.

What will you put in your nosebag or lunch box?

Bread comes in many flavors. Try different kinds—brown, date, graham, nut, oatmeal, raisin, rye, enriched white, or whole wheat.

Sandwich filling. For each sandwich, spread two slices of bread with softened butter, margarine, or mayonnaise. This acts as a shield to keep the filling from soaking through the bread and tastes good too. Spread the filling almost to the edge of one slice. For filling use egg salad, peanut butter, sliced or chopped meat, jelly or marmalade, or your own favorite. Fillings that are very juicy or wet do not pack well because they soak through the bread.

Fruits and Vegetables. Apples, oranges, and celery pack well and are good when you are thirsty. Peaches, pears, plums, tomatoes, and grapes are also thirst quenchers, but they bruise easily so put them at the top of your nosebag. Bananas go on top, too. Stewed fruit in small jars with tight-fitting covers can go in a lunch box. Remember to put in a spoon. Chewy dried fruits, such as raisins and dates, make good nibblers. Take raw vegetables and cut them into small pieces. Cut carrots and cucumbers into strips, radishes into quarters. Remember to pack salt if you like it.

Desserts. Pack cookies, gingerbread, cake, dried fruit.

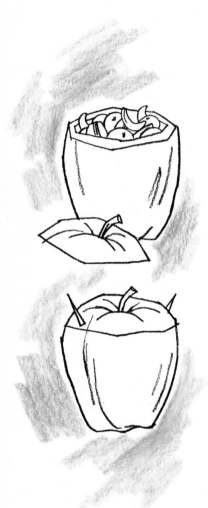

Beverages. A cool drink tastes good on a warm day and a warm drink is good on a cool day. Fruit juice, milk, cocoa, and soup can be carried in a vacuum bottle in a lunch box. Treat that vacuum bottle gently, it breaks easily.

Here is a salad you can eat on a hike.

WALKING SALAD FOR ONE

> 1 apple
>
> 2 tablespoons cottage cheese
>
> 5 or 6 raisins
>
> 2 or 3 nuts, chopped
>
> 1 teaspoon mayonnaise

1. Cut the top off the apple.

2. Core it almost all the way through leaving the bottom skin over the hole.

3. Scoop out the pulp of the apple and chop it up with cheese, raisins, and nuts.

4. Mix with mayonnaise.

5. Stuff the mixture into the apple shell and put the top on.

Starting To Cook

You can find recipes for all kinds of foods in cookbooks and on mix boxes. Some dishes are better for indoor parties, others better for cooking out-of-doors. You will find outdoor recipes in the Girl Scout cookbook *Cooking Out-of-Doors*.

Your grocer's shelves are stocked with every kind of mix—cakes, cookies, desserts, beverages, vegetables, soups. When you cook from a mix, follow the directions on the package, *exactly!* If you put too much water in or mix things in the wrong order you may be very disappointed in your punch or cookies or whatever you are making.

After you have used a mix, try making the same thing from a recipe. Measure out the ingredients and mix them yourself. It is more fun but it does take more time and more skill.

Before you start cooking from a recipe or a mix:

1. Wash your hands.

2. Read your directions or recipe.

3. If you are not sure how to follow certain directions ask your mother to explain them.

4. Collect all ingredients and equipment you are going to need, and line them up in front of you. Then you are sure before you start that you have everything you need. And you know that if you have anything left over, you forgot a step.

5. Know how to use the stove or oven or outdoor fireplace. Read about making fires in the chapter "Fires," and practice.

Ways To Cook

Boil — To heat liquid—not fat—to point where bubbles break. Use saucepan or kettle.

Stew — To boil slowly in any kind of pan.

Fry — To cook food in hot fat. Use skillet.

Pan Broil — To fry, pouring off fat as it accumulates Use skillet.

Sāuté or Pan Fry — To fry quickly in small amount of fat and turn gently. Use skillet.

Braise — To sauté food in fat and then cook it slowly—over low heat in small amount of liquid—on top of stove. Use skillet.

Steam — To cook food by the steam from boiling water. Use a double boiler, which is a pan of boiling water under a pan with the food in it.

Bake — To cook—cakes, pies, cookies, vegetables —in an oven.

Roast — To cook meat in an oven or in the coals of an open fire. Use open pan or wrap in foil.

Broil — To cook directly over hot coals or under the flame. Use grill for open fire and open pan or broiler and rack for oven.

Cooking Tips

Line a baking pan with wax paper instead of greasing it. Use wax paper baking cups to line muffin tins.

Pour cereals slowly into salted, boiling water.

When you cut apples for a salad, leave some of the peel on for a touch of color. If you are making salad, keep apples from turning brown by squeezing lemon over them as you cut or stir them into mayonnaise.

Cut butter into smooth squares by dipping knife into hot water before cutting or by putting wax paper over knife.

Use a paper bag to cover chicken, meat, or fish with flour or meal. Put the flour or meal with salt and pepper in a bag. Mix it up. Then add the cut-up chicken, meat, or fish. Close the top of the bag and shake gently.

Rinse egg or milk dishes in cold water before washing. Rinse sugar dishes in hot water.

Cut onions under cold running water to prevent tears.

Cook strong flavored vegetables—cabbage, onions, turnips— without a cover on the pot. This allows the odor to escape. Cook green vegetables without a cover to preserve their color.

Before you frost a cake dip the spatula into warm water and then dry it.

Wash your pots and pans as you go along so that you will not have a sink full of dirty dishes waiting for you. Use as few utensils as you can.

Measuring

A recipe tells you how much of each ingredient to use. It is up to you to measure *exactly* the amount called for. If the recipe calls for a teaspoon of vanilla and you put in a tablespoon—that is three times as much—your cookies will taste strange. If the recipe calls for one cup of flour and you put in almost but not quite a cup, your cake will disappoint you. Good cooks know that the secret of cooking success is measuring accurately.

But suppose you need twice as much food as the recipe makes. If the recipe serves four people and you need enough for eight people, you will have to make twice as much. Perhaps your recipe cannot be doubled. Then you will have to make two batches. If the recipe can be increased—ask an experienced cook about your recipe—then you multiply the amount of the ingredients by two.

When you increase a recipe you need to know that several small measurements make one large measurement—two cups make one pint. When you plan your shopping list you will need to know these measures and equivalents. You cannot buy two cups of sugar but you can buy one pound of sugar and that is the same amount. If you want to buy enough milk for cocoa, look at your recipe. It says that you need four cups of milk. You cannot buy milk in cups, but you see by looking at the measures on the next page that four cups of milk equal one quart. You buy one quart.

MEASURES AND EQUIVALENTS

3 teaspoons	=	1 tablespoon
16 tablespoons	=	1 cup
2 cups	=	1 pint
4 cups	=	1 quart
16 cups or 4 quarts	=	1 gallon
1 tablespoon of butter	=	½ ounce
8 tablespoons of butter	=	4 ounces or 1 stick of butter
2 cups of butter	=	1 pound or 4 sticks of butter
3 tablespoons of cocoa plus 1 tablespoon of butter	=	1 ounce or square of chocolate
1 cup of uncooked rice	=	3 cups of cooked rice

Safety Tips

In your kitchen—indoors or outdoors:

Keep knives and other sharp utensils in a separate section of a drawer or rack so people will not get cut when they reach for another utensil.

Turn pot handles away from the edge of the stove so no one will bump the handle and cause the pot to spill.

Keep curtains, towels, pot holders, your clothes and hair away from flames.

Clean up at once anything that spills or breaks, so no one will slip or get cut on sharp edges.

Before you leave a kitchen be sure the stove and electrical appliances are turned off.

If young children are around, be sure cleaning supplies, matches, all harmful things are always out of their reach.

If a fire starts in a pan on the stove, turn off heat and then smother the fire with a lid or pour baking soda on the flames until the fire is out.

Science in Cooking

Why do some baked foods—breads and cakes—rise? What happens from the time you mix something to the time you take it out of the oven?

Bread rises because it has yeast in it. If you do not put yeast in bread you get flat or unleavened bread. You cannot see yeast. What you see when you put yeast in the bread mixture looks like cheese or like a powder. Yeast is in that food but is invisible to the eye. Yeast is a plant and gives off carbon dioxide, a gas, when bread dough is put in a warm place. The carbon dioxide bubbles make the bread rise.

To watch this happen, get a ball of yeast dough from someone who is making bread. Place that ball of dough in a bowl over a pan of steaming hot water and watch it grow bigger.

Cake rises too, but not until it gets in the oven. Why? Discover for yourself in these kitchen experiments.

PLAIN CAKE

What happens to cake batter when it gets in the warm oven? This experiment will help you understand what happens.

You need: Two cups or custard dishes, cream of tartar, baking *soda*, baking *powder*, water.

1. Label the two cups or dishes A and B.
2. Measure ½ teaspoon cream of tartar into A.
3. Measure 1 teaspoon baking *powder* in B.
4. Add ⅓ cup warm water to A and see what happens.
5. Add ⅓ cup warm water to B and see what happens.
6. Add ¼ teaspoon baking *soda* to A and see what happens.

You saw that the mixture in B fizzed but the mixture in A did not—until you added the baking soda. Why did one mixture fizz when the other did not? Well, the fizz is caused by carbon dioxide gas bubbles being released. That happens when three things get together—an acid, a base, and warm water.

Now the baking powder in cup B had two of those things already in it—an acid and a base. So when warm water was added, carbon dioxide, a gas, was formed and it fizzed.

The cream of tartar in cup A had only an acid in it—no base— and so it did not fizz when water was added. To make it fizz you added a base—baking soda. When you added it to the cream of tartar and water, you had the three elements you needed. Carbon dioxide was formed and it fizzed.

Those carbon dioxide bubbles make a cake rise. When you put a cake in a hot oven the bubbles stretch the batter. The only way the cake can go is up, so the cake rises.

ANGEL FOOD CAKE

Angel food cake is made without any base. How can an angel food cake rise then? This experiment will help you understand.

You need: A small balloon.

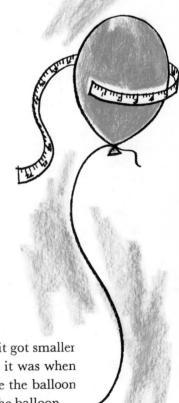

1. Blow up the balloon and measure it with a tape.

2. Put it in a cold place—outside if it is a cold day, in the refrigerator if it is not.

3. Leave it in the cold place for half an hour and then take it out and measure it.

4. Put the balloon close to something hot, like a light bulb. Then measure it.

What has happened? When the balloon got cold it got smaller When it was placed near heat it got bigger than it was when you first blew it up. The heat made the air inside the balloon get bigger—it expanded. Then the air stretched the balloon.

That is the trick to an angel food cake. It has air in it. When the cake is mixed, air is whipped into it. When this is put into the oven, the heat makes the air in the cake mixture expand, and that stretches the cake and makes it rise.

It is the heated air that makes the angel food cake rise.

137

Tasty Toasts

You can make toasts in the broiler of your kitchen stove or a toaster, or outdoors over hot coals. All you need are toasting sticks, bread spreads, and hot coals.

If you are toasting out-of-doors, you can use green sticks or lay bread over a wire grill. You also can make a toaster from a piece of heavy wire or a wire coat hanger. Wire toasters become hot, so use a pot holder.

Raisin, white, or whole wheat bread makes good toast. Toast with a spread is good for breakfasts, snacks, or desserts.

TOAST SPREADS

Applesauce Toast   Spread a generous layer of applesauce over hot buttered toast.

Cinnamon Toast   Mix cinnamon and sugar and sprinkle over buttered toast.

Orange Toast   Moisten sugar with orange juice and mix with grated orange rind and spread on toast.

138

Apricot-Marsh-mallow Toast   Make the apricot spread. Make it in advance and store it in a jar until you are ready to use it.

1. Soak half pound dried apricots overnight. Stew in same water, till tender.

2. Drain the water.

3. Press apricots through a sieve.

4. Add four tablespoons of sugar and heat the mixture.

Spread on buttered toast. Place a marshmallow in the center of each piece and toast under a broiler until the marshmallows are brown.

Bread Twists   Follow the recipe on a box of biscuit mix. Pinch off a fistful of the dough and mold it into a long patty. Wrap it around the end of a one-inch thick stick in a spiral twist. Put a piece of dough over the end of the stick and pat the cracks together. Toast over hot coals. The inside will bake as the outside toasts. Slip the bread twist off the toaster and fill the hole with butter, jam, or jelly.

Toasting tip. It is easy to burn a marshmallow or piece of toast. The good cook has patience and toasts food golden brown over slow, glowing coals.

SOMEMORES

It is easy to guess how these got their name. The food is so good you are certain to want "some more."

You need:

⅓ of a 1½ ounce bar of milk chocolate

2 graham crackers

1 marshmallow

1. Make a sandwich of the chocolate and the 2 crackers.
2. Toast marshmallow to a golden brown.
3. Put it into sandwich between chocolate and crackers.
4. Press gently together and eat.

You can make other Somemores.

* Use peanut butter or toasted peanuts instead of chocolate. These are sometimes called "Robinson Crusoes."

* Use slices of apples instead of crackers. These are "Apple Somemores."

* Use chocolate covered crackers and no chocolate bars.

* Use chocolate peppermints instead of chocolate bars.

One-Pot Meals

One-pot meals are easy to make and clean up after. Here are two one-pot meals. Look for others in cookbooks.

If you are going to cook over an open fire, rub the outside of your kettle or saucepan with liquid soap. Then the black from the flames—carbon—will come off easily at cleanup time.

CAMPFIRE STEW
(8 servings)

Ingredients	Utensils
2 pounds hamburger	Kettle and soap
1 onion, peeled and cut in small squares	Stirring spoon
1 tablespoon fat	Knife
2 10¾-ounce cans condensed vegetable soup	Tablespoon
	Can opener
Salt and pepper	

1. Put fat in bottom of kettle.

2. Add salt and pepper to hamburger and separate hamburger into little pieces or make little balls of it.

3. Fry hamburger with the onion until the onion is light brown and hamburger is well browned all over.

4. Pour off excess fat.

5. Add vegetable soup and enough water or soup stock to prevent sticking.

6. Cover and cook slowly until meat is cooked through. Serve hot.

141

The Basic Four food groups

BLUSHING BUNNY (8 servings)

Ingredients	Utensils
2½ tablespoons butter or margerine	Kettle and soap
2½ tablespoons flour	Tablespoon
3 10½ ounce cans condensed tomato soup	Can opener Stirring spoon
⅓ pound cheese, cut in small squares	Knife
16 slices toast	Toasting sticks or grill
Salt and pepper	Hot pad or gloves

1. Melt butter slowly.

2. Blend with flour. Mix until all the lumps are gone.

3. Add soup just as it comes in can.

4. When thoroughly heated, add cheese. Stir gently until melted.

5. Add salt and pepper.

6. Serve on toast.

142

Planning the Meal

When your patrol plans the menu, each girl has a chance to suggest her favorite foods. Remember that your body needs different kinds of foods, not just desserts. Your body is like an engine, and food is the fuel that makes it go. The right foods are found in the Basic Four food groups. Plan each day's menu to include some food from each of the four groups.

In planning a meal ask yourself:

1. What foods are in season and what is the weather like? If you are cooking outdoors in hot weather, can you keep your meat and milk and butter from spoiling?

2. Will you have different tastes and colors in your menu? Have you something crisp, something soft, something wet, something dry, something sweet, something new?

3. Will religious observances affect the menu?

4. Do you have enough money to buy what you want? If not, can you substitute foods that cost less?

5. How long does your recipe take to prepare and cook? Can you fix part of your meal ahead of time?

6. If you plan to take foods on a trip, are you fixing foods that carry well and need little equipment?

Write down the menus and how many people you are going to feed. Then list what you need to buy and how much. Next list equipment you need for cooking and eating. From this make lists for shoppers, girls in charge of equipment, and cooks. Finally, make a kaper chart showing who will do what.

Shopping

Members of your troop can take turns shopping. Several Scouts can go together or you can go with your mother or another adult. Take your grocery list. Then you will not forget anything—unless you forget the list! At the store you will usually find several brands of one item, some more expensive than the others. Read the labels to see what you can find out about each brand. How much does the package or can contain —how many cups or ounces or servings?

Do not buy the "big bargain size" if you do not need that much.

A can of cut food is less expensive than a can of whole pieces. If your recipe calls for uncut pieces, then you must use them. If it doesn't, you can use the cut pieces and save money.

When you shop for a mix, be sure to read the label to see whether you will have to buy ingredients to add to the mix. Will you need an egg or milk?

Outdoor Kitchen

Your kitchen at home has a place to keep food, to work, to wash dishes. Outdoors you set up your own kitchen.

You need:

1. Shady and dry place to store food.
2. Safe place to build a fire.
3. Work place to prepare food.
4. Attractive place to eat.
5. Dishwashing spot.
6. Place or way to dispose of garbage.

Tie your nosebag on a clothesline tied between two trees. This will keep it dry and cool. Or take a rope and tie a rock in a bandana to one end. Toss the bandana over the limb of a tree —still holding on to the other end. Now tie nosebags or a pack basket to the rope.

145

Setting the Table

You set the table according to the menu and the way you are going to serve the food. There are different ways to serve.

Some families eat at the table and their plate is served to them with all the food on it.

Other families eat at the table but pass the food around in large dishes and serve themselves from those dishes. Sometimes the head of the family serves everyone.

Sometimes families eat buffet style which means all the food is put on the table and you serve yourself there, but you sit down to eat in the living room or outdoors.

The silverware and dishes you use to set a table depend upon the menu, the way the main dish will be served, and on the occasion—party or just family. You may not use all the dishes and silverware shown every day, but learn where they should be placed so that when these dishes are at *your* place, you know how to use them.

When you set the table, place napkins and place mats one inch from the edge of the table. Allow at least 20 to 24 inches for each place setting.

Cup and saucer. Right-hand side of plate, alongside of spoons.

Napkin. Left of the forks or underneath them. The lower right-hand corner should be the loose or open corner. It should open like a book.

Glasses. Upper right-hand side of point of knife. If iced tea or milk glass is used, place at right of water glass.

Silverware. Place the silver in the order the person will use it when he eats. Pieces to be used first go on the outside and pieces to be used last go on the inside.

1. Knife at right of place with cutting edge toward plate.

2. Forks at left of place with tines up. If a knife is not needed for the meal, place the forks at the right with the spoons.

3. Spoons at right of knife with bowls up.

4. Dessert silverware—spoon or fork—is often served with the dessert course. Place the spoon or fork at right, one inch from the edge of the table.

Salad plate. When the salad is served with the main course, place salad plate at the left of the forks. If a bread and butter plate is not used, place the salad plate in its place or just above the dinner plate.

Bread and butter plate. Upper left-hand side of plate. Place the butter spreader on the edge of the plate going the same way as the edge of the table. If you are using the bread and butter plate for salad, you can place the butter spreader on the table, above the dinner plate.

Serving the Meal

Serve and remove dishes from the left. Most people are right-handed and can serve themselves more easily if you hold a dish on their left.

Serve and remove beverages from the right so you will not reach in front of someone.

When you clear the table, first take away the serving dishes, salt and pepper, bread and relish tray. Then remove the dishes and silver. Never stack the dishes at the table. Scrape and stack them as soon as you take them to the kitchen.

When you are serving more people than can sit comfortably at a table, serve buffet style. The utensils and the food are placed on the table in a special way. The guests serve themselves but do not sit at the table. Usually the hostess pours the guests' beverages.

For a buffet meal, plan only food that does not have to be cut with a knife. It is very hard to cut meat when you have your plate on your lap.

150

Table Manners

A Girl Scout is courteous. Good table manners are a courtesy to other people at the table. Girl Scouts have good table manners.

Table manners are different in different parts of the world, but everywhere good manners are a way people show kindness and respect to one another.

This is how you show respect to your family and your friends.

1. Dispose of chewing gum before you sit down to eat. Wrap it in a piece of paper and throw it in a trash basket.

2. Chew your food with your mouth closed.

3. Do not talk when you have food in your mouth.

4. Wait to start eating until your hostess has started. At camp you usually wait for the leader to start to eat.

5. Sit up straight and help carry on a pleasant conversation.

6. If you use a teaspoon for stirring, put it down on a plate or saucer. Never leave a teaspoon in a cup, where it can upset the cup if it is bumped.

7. When you have finished your soup or dessert, leave the spoon on a plate.

8. When eating soup, dip the spoon away from you so it will drip over the bowl, not on your lap. Sip without noise from the side of the spoon.

151

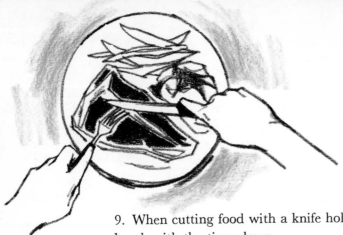

9. When cutting food with a knife hold your fork in your left hand, with the tines down.

10. Break bread into small pieces and butter one piece at a time, as you eat it. Never cut bread with a knife.

11. When passing your plate to the hostess for a second helping, place the silver near the center of the plate. Do not take the silver off and hold it or put it on the table.

12. Always leave the bread and butter spreader on the bread and butter plate or, if there isn't one, on the salad plate.

13. When the meal is over, partly fold your napkin and lay it at the left side of the dessert plate.

14. You may eat the following foods with your fingers: Carrot sticks, cabbage wedges, turnip strips, olives, radishes, corn on the cob, most raw fruits, small whole pickles, candied fruits, potato chips, breads, cookies. If you are not sure how to eat something watch your hostess and do as she does.

15. If food is being served that you do not like or that you have never tried before, ask your hostess for a small serving. People's taste in food changes, and what you did not like last week, you may find delicious this week. Girl Scouts in camp sometimes ask for "just three bites, please" or "just a taste, please," when they are not sure about a certain food. This is a way of being thrifty and also a way of trying out and getting to like a new food. Eating will be more fun when you get to like many different foods.

Dishwashing

Dishwashing can be done quickly if you know how. The picture clues can show you how to do a clean, quick job.

Leave a clean kitchen. Clean the sink, dispose of the garbage, and sweep up. Before you leave the kitchen, see that the oven and burners are turned off and everything is picked up.

Out-of-doors you use a bucket for a sink and you heat your own water, but you still scrape, rinse, and wash dishes. To sanitize dishes you put them in a dunking bag.

You can make your own dunking bag from two loosely woven dishcloths. Sew three sides of the dishcloths together and run a shoelace or cord through the top for a drawstring.

scrape   rinse   wash   scald or sanitize

drain   clean sink   sanitize   air dry

GAMES

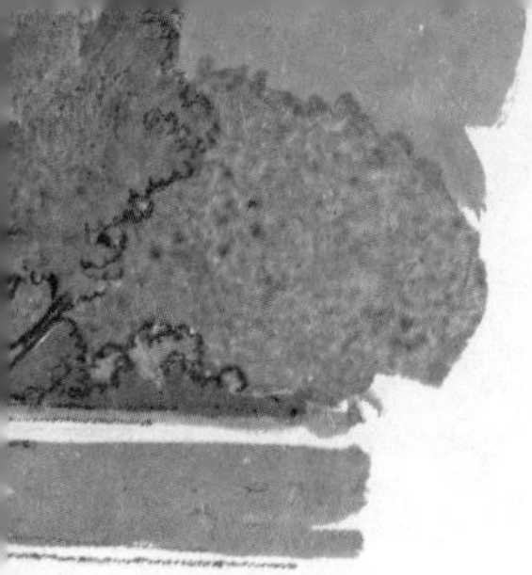

Dear Girl Scouts:

I hope that we shall all remember the rules of this Girl Scouting game of ours. They are:

To play fair,
To play in your place,
To play for your side and not yourself.

And as for the score, the best thing in a game is the fun and not the result, for:

"When the Great Recorder comes
To write against your name,
He writes not that you won or lost
But how you played the game."

Girl Scouts, I salute you.

Your friend and founder,

Juliette Low

There are different kinds of games.

* Running around games that leave players breathless. Run, Skip, Jump on page 157 is a good action game.

* Quiet games that give people a chance to catch their breath. Kim's Game on page 159 is a quiet game.

* "How much do you know" or "how fast are you" games that teach and also test how much players remember of what they learned at troop meeting. See Judging Contest on page 91, Wheel Whiz on page 158, String Burning Contest and Clothesline Relay on page 160, Rescue Relay and Dog Team Race on page 161, Signal Game on page 176.

* Singing and dancing games that mix music and dancing with a game and lead to folk dancing. "Skip to My Lou" on page 200 is one of these.

* Wide games (see pages 162-165) that take you all over your neighborhood or the countryside using your compass and map skills.

Pick a game that suits the occasion.

156

RUN, SKIP, JUMP

A lively game—an acting-out game.

1. Players take partners and stand in a double circle with one partner in each circle. The circles will move in opposite directions.

2. The game leader calls out commands for the first game. She changes the command every few seconds. Commands could be:

Walk as if:

* You were going down a camp path with a flashlight, carrying a bedroll, a big rock, a bird in a cage

* You had a puppy on a leash

* You were going down the aisle of a moving train

* You were skipping rope

* You were a duck, an elephant, a monkey, a rabbit

3. When the leader claps her hands, the players find their partners and squat.

4. The first set of partners to squat down take turns calling commands for the next game.

WHEEL-WHIZ

A game to try out or test your skill on wheels.

You need: Bicycles or roller skates and room enough to use them, paper cartons, judges.

1. With the paper cartons mark a course for players to follow on their bicycles or skates. Include as many safety rules and traffic signs as you can.

2. Riders or skaters take the course one at a time, with enough time between players so that there is no crowding. Each player covers the course as well as she can following signs and giving signals before turns.

3. Judges watch each player and give a point each time she hits a carton or goes off her course.

4. Player with lowest score wins.

I am turning right   turning left   stopping

Look at this for two minutes and then close the book. How many objects can you list?

KIM'S GAME

A quiet game to try out or test your powers of observation.

You need: Ten to twenty objects placed on a table, paper and pencil for each team.

1. Players study objects on table for two minutes.

2. When time is up the game leader covers up the objects and each team makes a list of the objects they remember.

3. The team with the longest correct list wins.

Objects for the game could be:

∗ All the things in a first aid kit

∗ Things to take on an overnight

∗ Food for a meal

∗ Different leaves or seeds or nuts

∗ Pictures of animals or flags or a jumble of different things

This game came from the story "Kim" written by Rudyard Kipling. In the story Kipling has the game used as an observation exercise for secret service agents in India. Kim's Game is a favorite of Scouts and Guides all over the world.

159

STRING BURNING CONTEST

Test your fire building skill (see "Fires" chapter).

You need: Two stakes—use straightened wire coat hangers—for each pair of players; a piece of string to tie between the stakes about a foot off the ground; small woodpile; matches; can of water to douse the fire.

1. At starting signal, each couple builds fire under string. Try allowing yourself only two matches.

2. First pair to burn through their string wins.

CLOTHESLINE RELAY

Test your clove hitch (see page 99).

You need: Two broomsticks or flagpoles or chairs or posts for each team; a rope, a bandana, or something to hang on the line for each pair of players.

1. Players on each team pair off.

2. First pair runs up to the sticks and puts up a clothesline, using a clove hitch. Then they hang their bandana on the line and run back to tag the second pair of players.

3. Second pair runs up and ties their line above or below the first one. Then they tag the next couple.

4. First team to finish wins.

RESCUE RELAY

Practice water rescue.

You need: A pole or beach towel for each team.

1. Two teams line up in shallow water and stand facing their captains on shore.

2. At a signal from the game leader, each captain holds out a pole or throws out the end of a beach towel to the first player and pulls her to shore.

3. First player climbs out and then "rescues" the second player in the same way. The second rescues the third and so on until all members on one team are pulled to shore.

4. The first team on dry land wins.

DOG TEAM RACE

Test your square knot or sheet bend (see pages 96, 98).

You need: Sled or wagon for each team; and five, six, or seven pieces of rope about four feet long for each team.

1. Players divide into groups of six or eight. One girl is the Driver and the others in her team are the Huskies.

2. Huskies line up at starting line in front of sled or wagon.

3. At starting signal, Huskies tie their ropes together. They use square knots or sheet bends to make a long rope. This is their Harness.

4. Driver climbs onto sled or wagon and holds one end of Harness. Holding other end, Huskies pull Driver on sled or wagon to finish line. If Driver falls off or ropes come untied before they reach finish line, team must return to starting line and begin again. First team to reach finish line wins.

Wide Games

A wide game is a special kind of Girl Scout game played by Girl Scouts and Guides all over the world. It is called a wide game because it covers a bigger area and lasts longer than other games.

It is a kind of a trail. It has a story or theme, and everything you do along the trail tells part of that story. The story or theme of your wide game will depend on the place where you play the game and the skills you would like to use.

You play a wide game at camp, in the city, in the woods, or even in a house. Wherever you play, that place becomes a trail with

adventure around each bend. To follow the trail you must use all your skills—observing, listening, smelling, map making, knot tying, fire building, cooking, reading directions and following them, first aid, history of Girl Scouting—everything!

The trail for a wide game is made up and laid by the Court of Honor or by a patrol. The trail can be followed by patrols or groups of two or three. Each group starts out along the trail at least ten minutes apart.

Here is a sample wide game. The theme of this wide game is Juliette Low's birthday.

Starting point: Team receives a note saying, "Juliette Low started Girl Scouting in the city of Savannah by a telephone call to her friend. Get your first clue by telephoning the number below. Mrs. Brown, a troop committee member will answer. Tell her who you are and ask her where you can find a daisy." Team calls Mrs. Brown.

1st point: Mrs. Brown tells Scouts where to find a person with a daisy. They find her. She also has a pumpkin. She says, "Juliette Low was born on Halloween so with your knife cut an eye or nose to start a Jack O'Lantern." Then she shows the team where the trail marked by little paper pumpkins starts and tells them to follow it.

2nd point: Two Scouts are stationed at end of the pumpkin trail. They say that Juliette Low liked to put on plays. They ask the team to choose and act out a Halloween ghost or clown. When they guess what the team is acting out, they make a trail sign to show the team which way to go.

3rd point: Along the path the team meets a person dressed as an Indian. She tells them that Juliette Low's grandmother was captured by Indians and lived with them. Her Indian name was Little-Ship-Under-Full-Sail. If the team can tell north by looking at the sun, the Indian will give them a sketch map to the next point. Team tells her which way north is and she gives them the sketch map.

4th point: The sketch map leads them to a person with an American flag. She says that the first Handbook was called *How Girls Can Help Their Country*. She asks team to tell her two ways a Girl Scout can be a good citizen on a hike. Then she asks them to fold the flag. She then directs them to a trail marked by red ribbons.

5th point: At end of trail a person meets the team and says that Juliette Low had friends all over the world. She asks team to show how they would greet a Guide from another country. What emblem would the Guide wear that the team also wears? Then she says that Juliette Low camped with many girls and was a good story-teller at campfires. Team receives directions that lead to a campfire and tell them what their part of the campfire is.

165

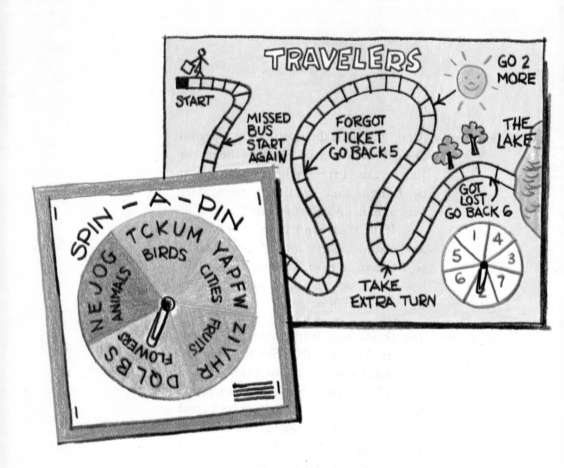

Make Up Your Own Games

It's fun to make up games and have other girls play them.

Kinds of games you can make up:

* Relay—where girls run and do something and then run back.

* Quiz games—where girls are asked questions about a subject they may know well or not so well.

* Circle games—where players change places.

* Observation games—where girls have to guess what is happening or what is wrong or missing.

* Team games—where each team tries to get something done before the others do.

What can you do in games? What have you just learned to do?

Here are some ideas. You will think of others.

* Signal a letter or word (see page 176).
* Put paper stars down in constellations.
* Give the Girl Scout sign or handshake (see page 24).
* Use words in another language (see page 177).
* Set a table (see page 148).
* Use a first aid skill (see pages 304-310).

Decide when you make up a game:

1. What the action or questions will be.

2. How the game will start and end.

3. What will be needed—equipment, judges, a starting and a finish line.

1

2

When you teach a game:

1. Get the players in position for the game. Tell them whether you want teams or circles. Have them count off for teams or take hands to form a circle. Tell where teams should line up.

2. Explain what you want the players to do. Let some players try the action so the others can watch and ask questions.

3. Tell the players how the game starts, how it ends, and who wins.

4. Have a clearly marked starting point and goal or finish line.

Draw or paste or cut out games. You can also make the kind of games a girl can play by herself. This kind of game is good at a party where girls take turns or as a gift to someone who is sick. Think of the kind of games you like.

Use what you can find around the house to make your game.

168

3   Can you "Name-it"? See answers below.

4

5

Cardboards from cut-up boxes or from laundered shirts are good for your "board" or for "Name-It" cards or for cards telling you to "go 2 spaces."

Markers can be made of buttons, stones, shapes cut out of cardboard.

Spinners can be made with safety pins or paper clips. Thumbtack the spinner to the board. If the thumbtack sticks out too far on the other side, add a piece of cardboard. Corrugated cardboard from cartons and thumbtack cards is good.

"Name-It" cards can be easily carried on a hike or given to someone sick in bed. Paste pictures of birds or animals or flowers or flags or Girl Guides on cards. Then on the back of each card, indicate what is on the front.

To play "Name-It," the game leader holds up the front of the card. The first girl or team to name it correctly gets a point. The one with most points wins.

5. Hummingbird
4. Blue Jay
3. Cardinal
2. Robin
1. Woodpecker

Games Parties and Play Days

One good way to make new friends is to invite other troops or camp units to a games party or a play day.

At a games party held in your troop meeting place or at camp on a rainy day, you can have table games in one part of the room, guessing games in another, and relays in the center of the room. Outside you can have fire building contests and games that need open spaces.

When you plan a play day or games party, answer these questions:

BEFORE THE PARTY STARTS

✳ What is your special part in the plan for the day? Does every member of your troop know what her part is and when and where to do it?

✳ If you want your guests to bring any equipment or be prepared with certain skills, tell them so when you invite them. Tell them how long the party will last.

THE ARRIVAL

✳ Who will meet the guests when they arrive?

✳ What will you do first—to break the ice? Will you sing or play a circle game with the entire group?

GETTING STARTED

* If you divide into groups, how will you get members of different troops or units mixed up in the groups? How will they meet each other? By colored name tags? A "mixing up" game?

THE GAMES

* Is there enough space and equipment for everyone to play the same game together? Or will it be better to divide into smaller groups, so players can rotate from one game to another?

* What games will you play? Who will be game leader for each game? Exactly where will each game be played and how much space will be needed for it? What equipment will be needed? Are you sure of the rules? Will you need judges?

* How long does it take to play each game? Should one group play two short games while another plays one longer game?

* Who will give the signal for the group to move on to the next game?

* Will each group need a hostess to show them where to go when they move to the next game? Or will there be signs in the games areas telling them where to go?

THE END OF THE PARTY

* How will you end the day? What time will your party end?

* What is your part of the cleanup?

SIGNALING

People signal messages to each other all the time.

You signal a message when you use words. When you smile or wave or make the Girl Scout sign to a friend, you are signaling. You can signal messages with pictures or with stones on a trail. You can signal with flags or flashing lights or whistles or drum beats.

Can you read this message?

···· / --- / -- / ·/ // - / --- // - / ···· / · //
···· / ·· / --- // ··· / ·-- / ---- / ···· / ··· //

It is written in Morse code.

INTERNATIONAL MORSE CODE

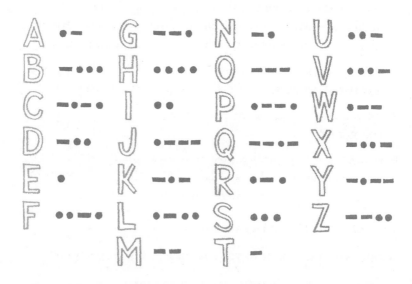

A	·—	G	——·	N	—·	U	··—
B	—···	H	····	O	———	V	···—
C	—·—·	I	··	P	·——·	W	·——
D	—··	J	·———	Q	——·—	X	—··—
E	·	K	—·—	R	·—·	Y	—·——
F	··—·	L	·—··	S	···	Z	——··
		M	——	T	—		

Signaling by Morse Code

Morse code is a system for signaling messages by dots and dashes. It is an international code and is used by people all over the world. The code was invented by Samuel Morse for the telegraph. A telegraph can send only sound—not voices. But, by using a long buzz for a dash and a short buzz for a dot, telegraph operators could use the Morse code to signal words.

The dots and dashes of the Morse code can be signaled with a flag or with sound or with light. Ships at sea use all three. Ship signalmen "talk" to each other with signal flags and blinker lights. You can "talk" to your friends with a flag or a bandana. You can talk with a whistle, a buzzer, a drum, a knock on the wall. You can even talk with a flashlight.

Until you learn the Morse code by heart, use this page in your *Handbook* to change your messages into code and to change the code you receive back into words.

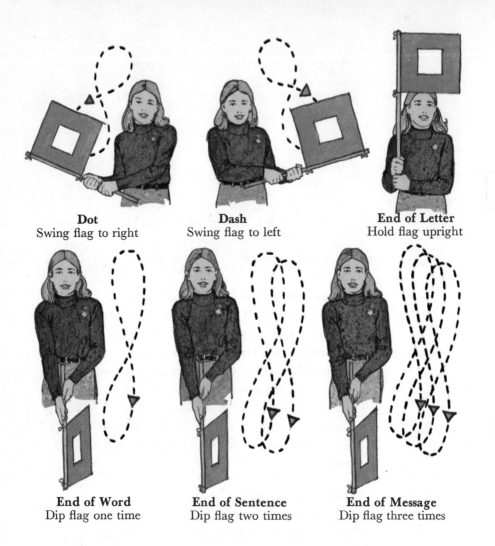

Dot
Swing flag to right

Dash
Swing flag to left

End of Letter
Hold flag upright

End of Word
Dip flag one time

End of Sentence
Dip flag two times

End of Message
Dip flag three times

MORSE CODE BY FLAG

In the daylight you can use a flag or bandana or handkerchief to send messages by Morse code.

Make your own signal flag. Take a square piece of cloth about two feet long on each side. Sew or glue on it a smaller square of another color cloth. Red and white are good colors for signal flags. A light color flag shows up well against a blue sky and dark trees or buildings. A dark flag shows up against a grey or cloudy sky and a light fence or wall.

174

MORSE CODE BY SOUND OR LIGHT

When it is dark you can signal with a flashing light. When it is quiet enough you can signal with a whistle or a buzzer. Here is the way you make the dots and dashes.

	Light	**Sound**
DOT	Short flash	Short blast or buzz
DASH	Long flash	Long blast or buzz
END OF LETTER	Short darkness (count 1)	Short silence (count 1)
END OF WORD	Long darkness (count 1-2-3)	Long silence (count 1-2-3)

HOW TO SEND MORSE CODE

Signal all the dots and dashes for one letter without stopping in between. A stop means the end of a letter.

To get the attention of the girl who is going to receive your message, send four A's (•−•−•−•−) without stopping.

When the receiver gets your ready-to-start signal, she signals back the letter K (−•−). That means, "OK. Start."

When the receiver wants you to repeat a word, she signals: IMI (••−−••). "I Missed It. Repeat."

When the receiver gets your message, she signals: T (−). "I understand."

To erase a mistake, signal: eight E's (••••••••). Then signal the word again.

To show that your message is finished, signal: AR (•−•−•).

HOW TO LEARN MORSE CODE

Start by memorizing these letters.

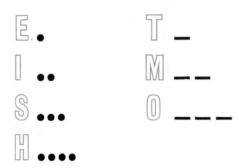

Baden-Powell learned E,I,S, and H—the four letters made only with dots—by remembering this sentence: "**E**nemy **Is S**ecretly **H**iding." He learned T,M,O—the dash letters—by remembering this sentence: "**T**ake **M**orse **O**rders."

How many words and sentences can you make with these seven letters? Here are a few words: Sit, hit, toot, tie, miss, seem, me, hot, meet. You can think of others. Practice sending and receiving these words until you know all seven letters by heart. Then work on the letters of your name.

Signal game. A good way to practice using Morse code is to play a game using the code. One player signals a word—using a flag, flashlight, or buzzer. The other players try to figure out—decode—the word. The first player to decode the word calls it out and scores a point for her patrol.

Signal teams. You can also practice in teams of four girls. Two girls are signalers. The other two are receivers. The two signalers decide what words to send. One signaler reads out from her *Handbook* the dots and dashes and pauses. Her partner signals them. One receiver watches the signaler and calls out the dots and dashes to her partner who writes them down. Then together they use a *Handbook* to decode the message.

Signaling in Other Languages

Signals like "Hello," "Thank you," "Please" can start friendships. But suppose you meet someone who speaks a different language from yours. How would you make your signal understood? You say friendship words in *her* language.

Here are some friendship words in French and Spanish and German and Japanese. Take attendance at a troop meeting by saying "Hello" in one of these languages. Then learn more words from people who know other languages.

French

Hello:	Bonjour	(Pronounce: *bohng-zhoor*)
Thank you:	Merci	(Pronounce: *mair-see*)
Please:	S'il vous plaît	(Pronounce: *seel voo pley*)

Spanish

Hello:	Hola	(Pronounce: *OH-lah*)
Thank you:	Gracias	(Pronounce: *GRAH-see-ahs*)
Please:	Por favor	(Pronounce: *pohr fah-VOHR*)

German

Hello:	Guten Tag	(Pronounce: *GOO-t'n tahk*)
Thank you:	Danke	(Pronounce: *DAHN-keh*)
Please:	Bitte	(Pronounce: *BIT-teh*)

Japanese

Hello:	Konnichi wa	(Pronounce: *KOHN-nee-chee-wah*)
Thank you:	Dome arigato	(Pronounce: *dohm ah-REE-gah-toh*)
Please:	Dozo	(Pronounce: *DOH-zoh*)

DRAMATICS

Everyone likes to pretend she is someone else once in a while. When you can make your friends see what you are pretending, then you are acting. You make people laugh or frown or think they are some place else.

There are many ways to act a character or something that happened. You can use just your body—no words. You can use both. You can use a puppet and speak the puppet's words. You can make shadows. But, however you act, you must think hard about your character if you want your audience to see him. All the things you remember about how people walk and move and talk will help you.

Pantomime

Pantomime is making people imagine what you are doing by the way you use your face, your hands, your body. You use no words and no costumes. Start by pantomiming for your patrol something you did that was exciting. See if they can guess what you are doing. Show by the way you act which of the five senses you use when you do these things:

* Pick a cactus blossom or a rose from a a thorny rosebush.

* Try to locate a strange scraping noise outside your tent.

* Find out if the airplane flying high overhead is a jet.

* Take a big bite of your favorite cake.

* Pass by a perfume counter in a department store.

Now do some of these things as another person would—a boy, a teenager, a glamorous lady, a policeman, an old person.

Voice

The way you say something tells how you feel about it. Take one idea—meeting someone or saying goodbye—and show how you would meet or say goodbye to:

* Your best friend.
* Your grandmother who lives in another town.
* Your favorite teacher.

Can your patrol guess whether you are excited or surprised or puzzled or sad or nervous?

Make a circle at a troop meeting, and experiment with the different ways you can say "Goodbye" or "Hello." One girl starts, and when the troop guesses how she feels, then the girl on her left has a turn, and so on around the circle. Use other words—"Oh," "Look," "Come in."

Monologue

A monologue is a play in which only one person speaks. All the other characters are imaginary and the audience must figure out what they are saying.

You can make up monologues yourself. For instance:

* Explain to the bus driver why you have no bus fare and then try to borrow the fare from another passenger.
* Try to convince your mother to let you borrow money from her for something she doesn't think you should buy.

180

A Play

A play must have characters, dialogue, and a plot. Something must happen to the characters in the beginning that makes the audience wonder, "What will happen next?" This is called suspense. Choose a story you remember or read one together.

COSTUMES AND PROPERTIES

For some plays you will need costumes and properties. Make them out of cardboard, squares of material, blankets, ribbons, bandanas, shawls, or scarves.

The way you wear your costume is important. You can show the audience whether your character is humble or proud, careful or careless—just by the way you wear your costume. The way you hold your properties—a big bag or a bent stick or a hot potato—can show whether your character is happy or angry, weak or strong.

Have you ever played Newspaper Costumes? Each patrol has a stack of newspapers and many straight pins. The patrols dress one or two of their members in newspaper costumes by tearing, rolling, fringing, and pinning the newspapers. The theme of costumes may be Halloween characters, characters from favorite songs, animals, whatever you wish. Then the girls in costume act out their characters and the others guess who they are.

Shadow Plays

You can put on a play using shadows for
characters. Actors dress up in costumes
and act out the story standing behind a
screen. Your costumes and properties
have to make sharp shadows but they do
not have to be real. A cardboard crown
makes just as sharp a shadow as a solid
gold one.

Hand Shadows

By using just your hands—and maybe your elbows—you can make shadow people and animals nod their heads, move their lips, blink their eyes, wiggle their ears. Watch to see how real animals and people move. If your fingers will not stay together when you want—put a rubber band around them.

183

Puppets

Puppets can act for you. You talk for them and make them move, but the audience sees only the puppets. Make puppet heads from clay, paper bags, potatoes, papier mâché, or this mixture.

You need: Wallpaper paste, sawdust, water.

1. Mix one part paste to five parts sawdust.

2. Add water to this mixture until it is as thick as dough.

3. Make it into a head shape and model the face. Make a hole for your finger.

4. Let the head dry.

5. Paint it. Glue on hair. Dress it.

Choral Speaking

We do not all sound alike when we speak, do we? Some people speak quite high; others quite low; and others, in-between.

Your voice can be played like a musical instrument. Try this experiment in your troop. Each take turns speaking these lines at a walking pace, as you might walk in the woods.

> *Take turns saying:* Walk on a rainbow trail
> Walk on a trail of song.
> *Second turns on:* And all about you will be beauty.
> *And third turns on:* There is a way out of every dark mist
> Over a rainbow trail.

Now, try it once more. This time group yourselves as best you can into high voices, medium voices, and low voices. The groups do not have to be evenly divided.

Separate the groups a little. By this time you know the lines. Together they make a chant of the Navajo Indian. Speak the chant together, quietly and naturally. The blend is good. How about the balance of sound? Did you feel that one group had too much strength? Then try standing "on the bias." Have the group that was least strong stand a bit in front. Medium strong, stand a little back of group I. Strongest, stand back of group II.

This is choral reading. Choral reading is good to use at Scouts' Owns and ceremonies, when you put on a program for guests, to open or close a meeting.

HIAWATHA'S CHILDHOOD

Henry Wadsworth Longfellow

All: By the shores of Gitchee Gumee,
By the shining Big-Sea-Water,
Stood the wigwam of Nokomis,
Daughter of the Moon, Nokomis.

Low:	Dark behind it rose the forest
	Rose the black and gloomy pine-trees,
	Rose the firs with cones upon them;
High:	Bright before it beat the water,
	Beat the clear and sunny water,
	Beat the shining Big-Sea-Water.
All:	At the door, on Summer evenings,
	Sat the little Hiawatha,
High:	Heard the whispering of the pine-trees,
Low:	Heard the lapping of the water,
All:	Sounds of music, sounds of wonder:
Solo 1:	"Minnie-wawa,"
All:	said the pine-trees,
Solo 2:	"Mudway aushka,"
All:	said the water;
High:	Saw the firefly, Wah-wah-taysee,
	Flitting through the dusk of evening,
	With the twinkle of its candle
	Lighting up the brakes and bushes;
All:	And he sang the song of children,
	Sang the song Nokomis taught him:

Solo 1:   Wah-wah-taysee, little firefly,
Little, flitting, white-fire insect,
Little, dancing, white-fire creature,
Light me with your little candle,
Ere upon my bed I lay me,
Ere in sleep I close my eyelids!

Low: Saw the moon rise from the water
Rippling, rounding from the water,
Saw the flecks and shadows on it,
Whispered,

Solo 1:   "What is that, Nokomis?"

All: And the good Nokomis answered:

Solo 2:   "Once a warrior, very angry,
Seized his grandmother, and threw her
Up into the sky at midnight;
Right against the moon he threw her;
'Tis her body that you see there."

High: Saw the rainbow in the heaven,
In the eastern sky, the rainbow,
Whispered,

Solo 1:   "What is that, Nokomis?"

All: And the good Nokomis answered:

Solo 2:   "'Tis the heaven of flowers you see there:
All the wild flowers of the forest,
All the lilies of the prairie,
When on earth they fade and perish,
Blossom in that heaven above us."

Low:	When he heard the owls at midnight, Hooting, laughing, in the forest,
Solo 1:	"What is that?"
All:	he cried in terror;
Solo 1:	"What is that?"
All:	he said,
Solo 1:	"Nokomis?"
All:	And the good Nokomis answered:
Solo 2:	"That is but the owl and owlet, Talking in their native language, Talking, scolding at each other."
All:	Then the little Hiawatha Learned of every bird its language, Learned their names and all their secrets,
High:	How they built their nests in Summer,
Low:	Where they hid themselves in Winter,
High:	Talked with them when'er he met them, Called them "Hiawatha's Chickens."
All:	Of all beasts he learned the language, Learned their names and all their secrets,
Low:	How the beavers built their lodges,
High:	When the squirrels hid their acorns,
Low:	How the reindeer ran so swiftly,
High:	Why the rabbit was so timid,
All:	Talked with them when'er he met them, Called them "Hiawatha's Brothers."

189

SINGING

At this very moment Girl Scouts and Guides are singing somewhere. In some part of the world the sun is setting and girls may be singing around a campfire. In another place, a troop may be singing as they hike, or serenading friends, or dancing. Another troop may be singing at a flag ceremony or Scouts' Own.

There are songs that greet a visitor or say goodbye. Songs tell stories about trips over mountains, across prairies, down rivers. They describe the sound of wind and frogs, birds and bells. Some songs are conversations, with questions and answers.

Girl Scouts sing many different kinds of songs—rounds, folk songs, art songs, patriotic songs. You can find hundreds of songs to sing in *The Girl Scout Pocket Songbook* and *Sing Together* and many other Girl Scout songbooks.

Rounds

A round is a short song that is sung in parts. "Row, Row, Row Your Boat" is probably one you know.

When your group learns a new round, sing the song all together all the way through until you know it well. Then, when you really know it, sing it in parts. If the song has three parts, your song leader divides the group into three sections. The girls in the first section start singing Part 1, and when they get to Part 2, the second section starts to sing Part 1. Then, when the second section gets to Part 2, the third section starts to sing Part 1. By that time the first section will be starting Part 3, Everyone will be singing. Each section follows the other round the song.

Here is a good round to sing at troop meetings.

WHENE'ER YOU MAKE A PROMISE

Four-part round

W. W. Shield

Folk Songs

Some songs were made up so long ago that no one knows who first sang them or when. They are called folk songs. Before there were any songbooks, mothers and fathers sang to their children songs they learned from their own parents. And when those children grew up they sang the same songs to their children. Each country has its own folk songs that tell how people lived and what they thought. Some songs are sad, many are funny. Some tell a true story, many tell a "tall" story. Here is a folk song from Switzerland.

GYPSY SONG

English version by V. M. S.

German Swiss Melody
Arr. by Charles Woods

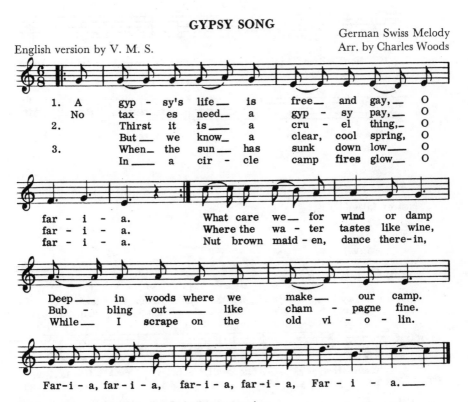

1. A gyp - sy's life __ is free __ and gay, __ O
No tax - es need __ a gyp - sy pay, __ O
2. Thirst it is __ a cru - el thing, __ O
But __ we know __ a clear, cool spring, O
3. When __ the sun __ has sunk down low __ O
In __ a cir - cle camp fires glow __ O

far - i - a. What care we __ for wind or damp
far - i - a. Where the wa - ter tastes like wine,
far - i - a. Nut brown maid - en, dance there-in,

Deep __ in woods where we make __ our camp.
Bub - bling out __ like cham - pagne fine.
While __ I scrape on the old vi - o - lin.

Far-i - a, far-i - a, far -i - a, far -i - a, Far - i - a. __

Faria: pronounce fair-ee-a. It has no meaning.

193

Songs for Special Occasions

At certain times Girl Scouts sing special songs. Before they eat a meal they sing grace. Here is one grace they sing.

A GRACE

Morn - ing
Noon - time } is here, the board is spread,
Eve - ning

Thanks be to God, Who gives us bread.

At the end of a troop meeting or a day at camp, Girl Scouts often sing Taps.

TAPS

Rukard Hurd
Slowly

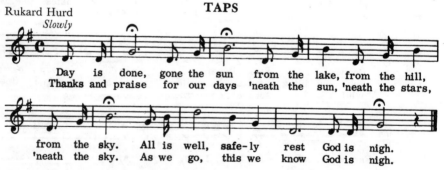

Day is done, gone the sun from the lake, from the hill,
Thanks and praise for our days 'neath the sun, 'neath the stars,

from the sky. All is well, safe-ly rest God is nigh.
'neath the sky. As we go, this we know God is nigh.

Words copyright by Pennsylvania Military College. Used by permission.
Daylight version approved by Lady Baden-Powell.

Art Songs

Some songs written by composers are called art songs. They are usually old enough to have stood the test of time. "Cradle Song" by Brahms, "Where E'er You Walk" by Handel, "Our Chalet Song" by Bovet are three art songs that Girl Scouts sing. Here is an art song you can learn.

THE EVENING STAR

Hoffmann von Fallersleben
Translated by Janet E. Tobitt

Robert Schumann

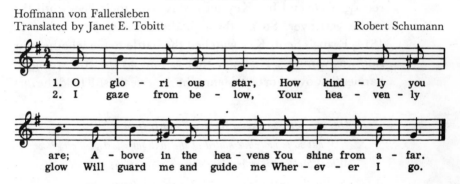

1. O glo - ri - ous star, How kind - ly you
2. I gaze from be - low, Your hea - ven - ly

are; A - bove in the hea - vens You shine from a - far.
glow Will guard me and guide me Wher - ev - er I go.

Patriotic Songs

There are songs that make you feel proud to be an American— "America the Beautiful," "O Beautiful Banner," "The Star-Spangled Banner." These are patriotic songs. Every country has its own patriotic songs and when its citizens sing those songs they feel proud, just as you do. The words are very important in a patriotic song. Do you know how the words were written for our national anthem, "The Star-Spangled Banner"?

195

STORY OF "THE STAR-SPANGLED BANNER"

Toward the end of the War of 1812, Francis Scott Key stood on a ship in the Chesapeake Bay watching a terrible battle. British ships were bombarding Fort McHenry. Key, a young Washington lawyer, had come to the British fleet to ask for the release of a captured friend. The British said they would release his friend but Key must stay with their fleet until the battle was over. So all through the night of September 13, 1814, Francis Scott Key watched the battle to see whether our side was winning. He knew that as long as the star-spangled banner flew over Fort McHenry the Americans still held the fort.

Oh, say, can you see, by the dawn's early light,
  What so proudly we hailed at the twilight's last gleaming?
Whose broad stripes and bright stars, through the perilous fight,
  O'er the ramparts we watched were so gallantly streaming.
And the rockets' red glare, the bombs bursting in air,
Gave proof through the night that our flag was still there.
  Oh, say, does that star-spangled banner yet wave
  O'er the land of the free and the home of the brave?

Toward morning, Key saw a flag flying over the fort. But which flag? Was it the British Union Jack or the American stars and stripes? In the dim light of the grey dawn, Key could not tell. Then the first rays of the rising sun shone on the flag. Yes! The star-spangled banner still waved!

196

On the shore dimly seen through the mists of the deep,
*   Where the foe's haughty host in dread silence reposes,*
What is that which the breeze, o'er the towering steep,
*   As it fitfully blows, half conceals, half discloses?*
Now it catches the gleam of the morning's first beam,
In full glory reflected, now shines on the stream;
*   'Tis the star-spangled banner; oh, long may it wave*
*   O'er the land of the free and the home of the brave.*

And where is that band who so vauntingly swore
*   That the havoc of war and the battle's confusion*
A home and a country should leave us no more?
*   Their blood has washed out their foul footstep's pollution.*
No refuge could save the hireling and slave
From the terror of flight or the gloom of the grave,
*   And the star-spangled banner in triumph doth wave*
*   O'er the land of the free and the home of the brave.*

Thankfulness swept through Key as he stood on that ship.

Oh, thus be it ever when freemen shall stand,
*   Between their loved home and the war's desolation;*
Blest with vict'ry and peace, may the heav'n-rescued land
*   Praise the Power that hath made and preserved us a nation.*
Then conquer we must, when our cause it is just,
And this be our motto: "In God is our trust";
*   And the star-spangled banner in triumph shall wave*
*   O'er the land of the free and the home of the brave.*

As these words came to his mind, he wrote them down on the
back of an envelope. Later, people liked his poem so much
they sang it and this became our national anthem.

DANCING

Ever since the world began people have always danced. Every country has invented its own kind of dancing. Today, when people travel more than ever, they bring home dances that started in other countries. When you watch television, movies, the stage, you see dances from all parts of the world.

But suppose a Girl Guide from Switzerland visited your troop and wanted to learn a dance from your country. What would you teach her?

Dancing the Crested Hen

Square dances and country dances are especially United States dances. These dances have steps from many countries because our nation was settled by people from all over the world. When our country was young, the settlers got together to dance after the work was done. They taught their dances to their neighbors. Square dance callers often made up calls and added their own ideas to the dances.

Here are two dances, one from our country and one from Denmark. Sing your own music and directions as you dance.

SKIP TO MY LOU

Dancers—"Gents" and "Ladies" form a circle with Ladies on the right of their partners.

1. Gents to the cen - ter skip to my Lou, Gents to the cen - ter skip to my Lou, Gents to the cen - ter skip to my Lou, Skip to my Lou, my dar - ling.

> *Action:* Gents skip to center and back to their partners.

2. Ladies to the center, skip to my Lou, (three times)
   Skip to my Lou, my darling.

   > *Action:* Ladies skip to the center and back.

3. Swing your partner, skip to my Lou, (three times)
   Skip to my Lou, my darling.

   > *Action:* Gents swing their partners.

4. Now to your opposite, skip to my Lou, (three times)
   Skip to my Lou, my darling.

   > *Action:* Gents swing ladies on the other side.

5. Promenade all and skip to my Lou, (three times)
   Skip to my Lou, my darling.

   > *Action:* Partners hold hands and walk around circle together.

6. Lost my lover, what shall I do? (three times)
   Skip to my Lou, my darling.

   > *Action:* Partners drop hands. Ladies keep going. Gents go in opposite direction.

7. Found another one just as true, (three times)
   Skip to my Lou, my darling.

   > *Action:* Gents reach out hands and take new partner. They promenade.

Denmark

Dance is done in groups of three — two "ladies" and one "man." Each set of three joins hands to form small circle. Sets of three make larger circle. Dancers step and hop on one foot, then step and hop on the other.

Join hands and cir-cle left, That's how to dance the Crest-ed Hen,

1. *Action:* Step hop in circle to the left.

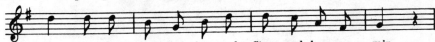

Step, hop, and step and hop and Step and hop a - gain.

2. *Action:* Continue to step hop in circle to the left.

Back now and cir-cle right, That's how to dance the Crest-ed Hen.

3. *Action:* Step hop in circle to the right.

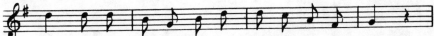

Step, hop, and step and hop and Step and hop a - gain.

4. *Action:* Continue to step hop in circle to the right.

Ladies drop each other's hand but keep hold of man's hand.

Right la - dy step and stir, Man fol - lows aft - er her,

5. *Action:* Man and lefthand lady hold up hands to make an arch. Righthand lady step hops under arch still holding man's hand. Man follows her.

Left la - dy step and stir, He fol - lows aft - er her!

6. *Action:* Man and righthand lady hold up hands to make an arch. Lefthand lady step hops under arch still holding man's hand. Man follows her.

7. Repeat number 5.

8. Repeat number 6.

When dance is repeated, man moves on to new set of ladies.

201

YOUR HOME

Your home may be an apartment in the city or a house near the sea, in a trailer on a farm, by a desert or tree.

Wherever it is, your home is more than just the rooms you live in. Your home is your family. Your home is where your friends visit, where you eat and work and play. Your home is where you give and take love and kindness every day. And you are an important part of your home.

Your Part

What is your part and how can you do it? The Girl Scout Law helps you. How many more ideas can you add to those below? Is saving water on your list? Practice good citizenship at home and conserve water. Try this experiment. Put a pan under a dripping faucet and see how much water collects in two minutes. There is probably enough to give your pet a drink. Do not be a water-waster!

Your Room—Your Own Special Place

Your room is your own special place. Here you sleep and entertain your friends. This is where you go when you want to be alone—to work, to read, to dream.

Your room shows the things you like and what you like to do. The books you read, your collections, the pictures on the wall, a plant you are growing, all add pretty touches to a room and are clues to the things you like.

Many girls share their room with a sister. Together they decide how to use the closet, drawers, the lamp. They share some things and have some of their own.

What is the first thing you see when you walk into your room? Most likely it is the biggest thing—your bed. An unmade bed makes the entire room look messy.

MAKE YOUR OWN BED

1. Smooth mattress pad. If you have a bottom sheet with corners sewn in, fit that over mattress. If you have a flat bottom sheet, center it on mattress so that you have an even amount hanging over at top and bottom and both sides. Tuck sheet under, first at top and then at bottom. Make square corners on each end. Tuck in sides.

2. Place second sheet on bed, wrong side up with wide hem at top. Leave enough sheet at top to fold down over blankets.

3. Put blankets on and fold sheet over them.

4. Tuck in blankets and second sheet together at bottom. Make square corners. Tuck sheet and blankets in along sides. Smooth.

5. Center spread on bed. Turn top down far enough to put pillow in. Smooth.

6. Lay pillow on bed and use both hands to pull on pillow case.

7. Put pillow at head of bed. Turn top of spread back over it. Smooth.

making a square corner

206

A PLACE FOR EVERYTHING

How much time have you wasted looking for a sock, a favorite handkerchief or pin, a pencil? A special place to put each thing makes it easy to find and keeps your room neat.

Paint boxes or cover them with pretty paper. Use a stencil or print to decorate. Spread a thin layer of glue on a lid and sprinkle shells, beads, or tiny pebbles over the wet glue. Make a box for your sister, too, if she needs a place to keep her things.

A laundry bag or hamper keeps dirty clothes out of sight until laundry day.

A wastebasket can be part of your room decoration. Pick out one of the colors in your room and paint the inside of a waste-basket or large can that color. Cover the outside with paper you have printed, a map, pretty wrapping paper, or use a stencil to decorate it.

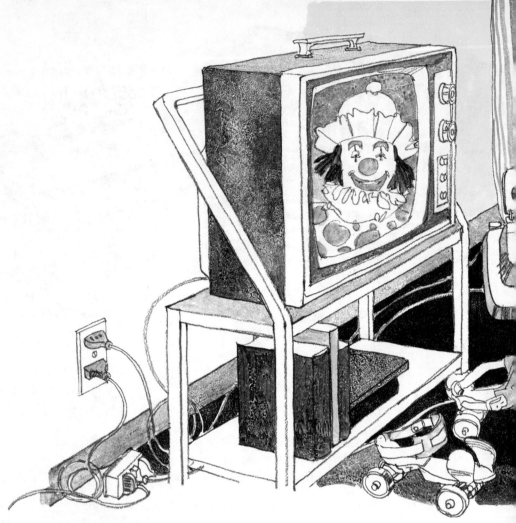

A Safe Home

Many accidents happen in homes. Most of them are caused by little things. What do you see in the picture which might cause an accident?

Safety projects a Girl Scout could do in this home:

* Make a toy box or game box for jacks, balls, roller skates.

* Make bottle label and ask her parents to help her mark it.

What other safety projects could she do in this house?

COLLECTING

Make a collection of things you like. Pick up shells from the
beach or leaves on a hike. Collect buttons or bells or many-
colored rocks. Or menus or maps or puppets made from socks!
Put snapshots in an album, arrange dolls on a shelf. Share your
hobby with others, work on it yourself. Arrange your collection, put it on view. Display it at a hobby show or to friends
who visit you.

Stories in Collections

Sometimes when you collect things, you find a story, too.

* What is the event that is honored on a stamp? If it is a person on the stamp, what did he do to be honored?

* What animal lived in a shell? How did it move? What did it eat?

* Do you have an old object in your collection? Who made it? Who did it belong to?

* Where did you find your objects? On a hike at camp? In your grandmother's attic?

* Where was a photograph taken? What was going on?

Adding to Your Collection

Do not keep your collection a secret! Ask people with collections or hobbies like yours for ideas. A collector is always glad to find a friend interested in the same hobby. Ask for tips on where to find items and how to display them. It makes a person feel good when you ask for help. You show that you think she has good ideas. A Cadette Girl Scout or Senior Girl Scout may be able to give you good tips. Tell all the girls in your troop what you are collecting. They may have ideas and items for your collection. You may add to their collections, too.

Keep your eyes open everywhere you go. A hike in the woods or along the beach may take you to new treasures. A friend may receive an interesting stamp on a letter. Of course you ask for permission before you take something—a stamp from someone else's letter or a menu from a restaurant.

Make trips to museums and exhibits. There you can see other people's collections and other ways to display things.

Visit libraries and book stores. Tell the librarian or clerk what your collection is. Ask what books he would suggest that you look at.

Trade with another collector. If you have several items alike, you can trade one with another collector for something different.

Meet collectors in your town. Look for them in hobby clubs, classes in a museum or community center, walks with a park naturalist.

Arranging Your Collection

Arrange your collection the way you like best. You might label each item. Or you might make groups of items. You can group by

* Size—big dolls together, little dolls together.

* Color—red rocks, green rocks.

* Style—new and old.

* Topic—stamps about animals, stamps about famous people.

* Places—coins grouped by the country from which they came or by countries where there are Girl Guides and Girl Scouts.

Your collection can be arranged to tell about things you have done. Menus from restaurants where you ate food of other countries could be arranged by food— French or Italian or German. On each menu circle the food you ate.

WHAT TO WEAR

What shall I wear? Shall I wear clothes for the sun or clothes
for the rain? What is right for a hike, or a trip on a train?

To find the answer, look at the sky and listen to the weather
report. Then ask yourself, "What will I do today?"

The Right Clothes

If you are going to a Girl Scout event, your uniform is your answer. If you are going to a party, your invitation or hostess often tells you what to wear. If you are going hiking through fields and woods, knee socks or slacks will protect your legs. If you will be cooking, an apron keeps your dress clean and a ribbon keeps your hair out of food.

KEEPING COOL

1. Keep the sun's hot rays from hitting your head and body. Wear a hat with a brim on a hike in the sun. Take a shirt to keep the sun from burning you at the waterfront.

2. Wear clothes that are loose so the air can get to your skin. Why? On hot days you perspire. If the air can get through your clothes, it causes the perspiration to evaporate and makes your skin feel cool. Put some drops of water on your arm. Your arm feels cooler where the water evaporates. Clothes that fit tightly, or are tightly woven, do not let air reach your skin. Perspiration cannot evaporate and you feel hot.

KEEPING WARM

1. Keep warm by wearing clothes that hold in the warmth of your body. Puffy, woolly materials do this because they have air in their thickness. Air is like a wall. It holds the heat of your body in and keeps the cold air out. Many layers of clothes are warmer than one thick layer because there are layers of *air* between each.

Try this experiment. You need a small piece of wool cloth and one of cotton cloth and two glasses of water. On the water in one glass lay the piece of wool. On the water in the other glass lay the piece of cotton. Look for little bubbles around the wool. These bubbles are air that was in the puffy wool. The air in the wool keeps it afloat longer.

2. Keep dry. Boots and water-repellent clothes keep you dry. On a camping trip, change to dry clothes when you go to bed because your day clothes will be damp from perspiration—even if you were not hot. And when the moisture from your day clothes evaporates, it makes you cold. Take off your boots indoors. If you wear boots indoors, your feet perspire and your socks get damp.

218

3. Keep the cold wind away from your body by wearing jackets and other clothing that will not let the wind through. Wind chills the warmth of your body. Clothing made of tightly woven material will protect the warm air held in the layers of clothing. A light jacket worn over two sweaters may be warmer than a heavy coat worn with no sweaters if it is windy. Experiment with your own clothes to see which combination is warmer.

GOOD FOOTING

On dry days, tiny bumps and hollows on the soles of your shoes catch against little rough places on the ground. This catching is called friction. Friction keeps you from slipping. But when water, ice, and snow fill up those rough places and make them smooth, there is no friction. Walking is slippery.

When the ground is slippery, a rubber sole can bend to form little creases that catch and hold your feet steady. Some shoe soles have ridges to keep you from slipping. Which shoes do you have that would be good to wear in wet weather?

Washing and Ironing

What happens in your house when the thing you want to wear next day is not clean? If you know how, you can wash it yourself. You can wash it in a sink or a washing machine if your mother lets you use it.

To wash most clothes, use lukewarm water and enough soap or other detergent to make the water sudsy. Squeeze suds through your clothes. Rub any spots. Rinse twice to be sure all the suds and dirt come out. Gently squeeze out the water, and hang your clothes up to dry. Use wood or plastic hangers or hang clothes over a rope. Do not use metal hooks or hangers. They may cause rust spots.

At camp you need to wash clothes sometimes. Even if you do not have hot water at camp, you can use cold water and wash in a bucket or basin. Pack soap at home in a plastic box or bag, so it will not spill in your duffel bag.

Before you begin ironing, ask your mother if it is necessary to dampen any of the clothes. Make sure the indicator on the iron is turned to "off" when you plug in the iron. Unplug the iron whenever you have to leave the ironing board. A steam iron should be unplugged when you fill it with water.

Start with the clothes that require a cool iron. When you work on a blouse, begin with the parts that show the most—the collar, cuffs, and sleeves. Hang up ironed clothes in some place where they can dry thoroughly. If clothes are crowded into the closet or put away still damp, they will wrinkle.

When you have finished your work, turn the iron to "off" before you unplug it. Set the iron to cool some place where it cannot fall over or burn anything.

Sewing

Learning to sew is one way a Girl Scout can learn to Be Prepared. Be prepared to sew on a button, mend a hem, sew your badges on your badge sash.

SEWING BOX

Keep your equipment together in a sewing box you made yourself. The box should be large enough to hold several spools of thread, a package of needles, a thimble, a small box of pins, and a pair of scissors, a tape measure, and a pincushion. A candy or shoe box makes a good sewing box. You can paint the box or cover it with fancy paper or cloth.

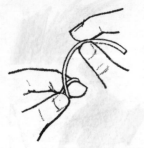

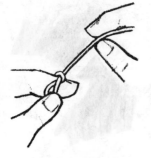

NEEDLES AND THREAD

Needles come in many sizes. Darning needles are long and have big eyes. Yarn needles have big eyes too, and blunt tips. Sizes are numbered. The higher the number is, the finer the needle. A number 8 needle is good for general use.

Thread also comes in numbered sizes. High numbers are thin threads. Low numbers are thick. Number 50 thread is good for general use. Use cotton thread on cotton, wool, and linen cloth. Use silk thread on silk and satin. Use nylon thread on most synthetic materials.

After you have threaded the needle, make a knot in the end of your thread. To make a knot, wrap the end of the thread around your first finger. Pushing with your thumb, roll the thread off your finger and tighten the knot by pulling the end of the thread.

To end sewing without making a knot, take several small stitches close together. Slip your needle under the last stitch. Pull it through, then cut the thread.

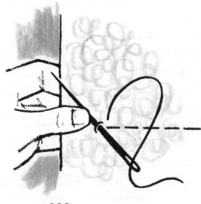

To hold two pieces of cloth together while you sew, pin as shown in basting picture. Use a thimble to sew heavy fabrics.

STITCHES

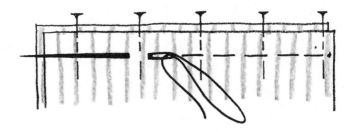

Basting A basting stitch is not a permanent stitch. It is a large stitch used to hold pieces of material together while you fit, stitch, or press. Baste before you sew a seam or hem.

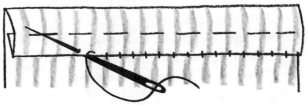

Hemming To put a hem in a skirt or a scarf, use this hemming stitch. Keep the stitches small and even. Use this stitch to sew your badges to your badge sash.

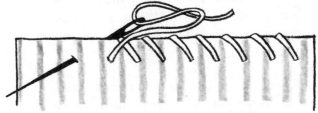

Overcast This stitch is used to finish cut edges of seams, to fasten two edges together or to decorate.

223

BUTTONS

Sew buttons on heavy materials—such as a coat—with a thread shank. First mark the place where the button is to go. Do this with crossed pins or a pencil mark. Knot the end of your thread. Take the first stitch down, leaving the knot on top where the button will cover it. Bring the thread up through one hole of the button and down through the other hole. Now insert a pin or heavy darning needle between the thread and the button as the picture shows. Sew over the pin four or five times. Remove the pin and pull the button away from the material. This leaves space to form the shank. Wind the thread around and around the threads between the button and the material. Pull the needle through to the underside and fasten the thread.

When you sew buttons onto thin material, you do not have to make a thread shank. Sew up and down through the holes a few times until the button is secure. Finish on the underside and fasten the thread.

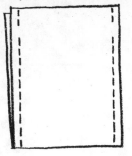

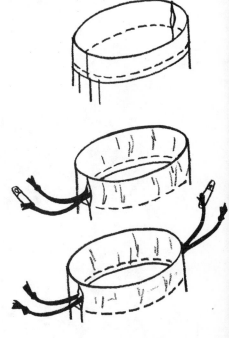

DRAWSTRING BAG

Use it: To carry your *Handbook*, pencil, paper, lunch, a snack for a hike.

You need: For the bag—a piece of sturdy, washable material 12 inches wide and 30 inches long, small safety pin, needle, and strong thread. For the ties—2 pieces of thin rope 36 inches long.

1. Fold the material in half with the wrong side out. Pin and baste a seam up each side. Leave a 1-inch opening in the seam about 2 inches from top. Sew.

2. Turn top edge down ½ inch. Baste.

3. Turn top down another 1½ inches. Pin and baste along edge of hem. Sew.

4. Turn the bag right side out.

5. Put safety pin through one end of a tie rope and push it through the opening. Push it around the top and out again where it went in. Tie ends together with square knot. Push the other rope through from the other side. Tie ends together.

6. To make a shoulder bag: Sew a strap and sew a loop on each end of it. Tie ropes from bag through loops in strap.

Juliette Low's Birthplace as it looked when she lived there.

FRIENDS

One way to keep old friends and make new ones is to do things together. Have a homemade ice cream party, a games party, a campfire. Go berry picking or sledding or visit an interesting place together. Invite another troop or camp unit to do one of these things or to a cookout or a hike. Invite parents and other people who helped your troop to a Court of Awards or picnic. Ask Brownies to come to a Court of Awards, a cookout, a play.

Before you get together, decide who you are going to invite and what you are going to do. Who will write the invitations? What food and decorations do you need? Who will get the refreshments ready? Which girls will be hostesses and meet the guests? Who will announce the games and activities? How will you end the day? How will you tell your guests you are glad they came? Make a kaper chart with everything to be done and who will do it.

227

Invitations tell guests when to arrive and where to come, how long the party will last and what to wear. RSVP—initials for the French words *Répondez s'il vous plaît*—on an invitation means "answer please" and the name and address or telephone number tell guests to whom to reply.

Friends in the U.S.A.

Girl Scouts from all fifty states can meet other Girl Scouts at three special places—Juliette Low's Birthplace, Rockwood, and national headquarters. If you live nearby, your troop can visit these places now. If you live farther away, when you are a Cadette Scout you can visit with your troop.

JULIETTE GORDON LOW BIRTHPLACE

If you live near Savannah, Georgia, you can visit the house where Juliette Low lived when she was a girl. You can see where she had parties for her friends, where she liked to read in front of the fireplace. If your family is traveling to Savannah, you can stop to visit the Birthplace. It is located at 142 Bull Street, Savannah, Georgia.

ROCKWOOD

At Rockwood, a Girl Scout program center in Maryland, troops and families from many states meet. Girls do not go to Rockwood by themselves, they go with their own troop or family. There, Scouts hike with girls from other parts of the country and trade ideas about things to do in troop meetings. Most of them go sight-seeing in Washington, D. C.

—only fifteen miles away. For more information about this program center, contact your Girl Scout council office and ask for a Rockwood folder.

GIRL SCOUT NATIONAL HEADQUARTERS

If you live near New York City or are traveling there, you can visit the national headquarters of Girl Scouts of the U.S.A. at 830 Third Avenue. Your troop is registered there with troops from all over the United States. Your uniform and badges are designed there. *American Girl* magazine is published there. Your *Handbook* is written there. Part of your membership dues helps to get these things done.

Friends Around the World

There are four special places where Girl Guide and Girl Scout friends from all over the world can meet—Olave House, Our Cabaña, Our Chalet, and Sangam. Each of them belongs to all Girl Guides and Girl Scouts. Perhaps you may visit one of them someday. The things you learn as a Junior Girl Scout can help you be prepared for such a visit. At these houses, everybody becomes a member of a patrol along with girls from different countries. When you learn songs, games, dances, and crafts, you are learning to share with girls from other countries. Sometimes events are carried out in another language. The languages you study in school will help you understand your new friends.

229

OLAVE HOUSE

Olave House is in London, England and Girl Guides and Girl Scouts stay there while they explore London. At mealtimes Girl Scouts and Guides tell what they do in their troop meetings, how they celebrate holidays, where they go camping.

OUR CABAÑA

Our Cabaña is near Cuernavaca, Mexico. Girl Guides and Girl Scouts who stay there can explore the palace in Cuernavaca and listen to the Indian legends about the mountains that surround Our Cabaña. Each year the Thinking Day tree near the front door is covered with white blossoms on February 22nd, the birthday of both Lord and Lady Baden-Powell.

OUR CHALET

Our Chalet near Adelboden, Switzerland is high in the Alps. There Girl Scouts and Girl Guides cook meals for each other using recipes from home. They dance the folk dances of their

Our Cabaña

countries. They learn how to tie ropes for mountain climbing and they hike along mountain trails.

SANGAM

Sangam is in the hills of India, near the town of Poona, where it is springtime all year. "Sangam" is an old Sanskrit word that means "coming together" as do small rivers flowing into one main stream. At Sangam, girls and adults meet, live, and carry out Girl Scout activities together.

THE UNITED NATIONS

In New York City, men and women from many countries come together at the United Nations building. Some of the people are delegates from nations. A delegate represents the government of his nation. The United States of America is a member of the United Nations and our delegate meets delegates from other countries. This is a way people representing nations get together.

ARTS WITH YOUR HANDS

Explore the arts. There's so much to do! Make a village of wood or a wonderful zoo. Print a leaf or a fern, weave a belt on a loom. Paint a picture and hang it somewhere in your room. Build a high flying kite, mold a figure of clay. Make a giraffe or a zebra of papier mâché.

In this chapter there are many kinds of art for you to try.

232

You will find more suggestions for things to make, tools to use, materials to try out when you read badge requirements.

When you choose a design for something you make, choose a simple shape. Look at the designs in the picture above. When you are the artist, you are free to make your own design the way you like it best.

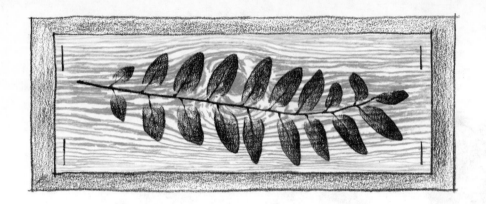

Use prints and stencils to make invitations, greeting cards, note paper. Decorate scrapbooks, your patrol flag, an apron, a storage box. Mount and hang prints in your room.

TRANSFER PRINTS

You can print leaves, ferns, grasses, feathers, unpainted wood, corrugated paper, so many things.

You need: Something to print, pane of glass, newspapers, paper to print on, oil-based printer's ink, brayer (roller) to spread the ink, spoon; rags or paper towel and turpentine for cleaning up.

Experiment with a leaf:

1. Cover your work place with newspaper. Place leaf on newspaper, vein side up.

2. Ink your brayer. Squeeze small amount of ink onto pane of glass. Push brayer over the glass until brayer is evenly covered with ink.

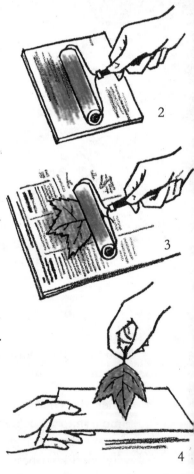

234

3. Roll the inked brayer over the leaf two or three times.

4. Lift the leaf and slip a clean sheet of newspaper under it.

5. Take the sheet of paper you want to print and carefully place it on top of the inked leaf. Try not to move the paper after it is down. Moving blurs the print. Fold a piece of newspaper and lay it on top of the print paper.

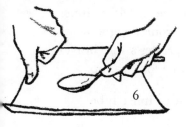

6. With one hand hold down the papers so they cannot slip. With the other hand rub the back of the spoon over all of the newspaper—up and down, back and forth. Rub every inch of the paper.

7. Remove the newspapers and gently lift the paper you printed.

8. Now make a print using other leaves or grasses. When materials become crushed, use new materials.

9. As soon as you finish printing—before the ink hardens—clean your hands, the brayer, and the pane of glass.

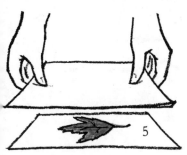

235

BLOCK PRINTS

You need: Pane of glass, newspapers, piece of felt or inner tube, scissors, block of wood the size of your design, white resin glue, paper to print on, oil-based printer's ink, brayer (roller); rags or paper towel and turpentine for cleanup.

1. Cut a simple shape from a piece of felt or inner tube.

2. Glue this shape to the top of the wood block. Let dry.

3. Squeeze a small amount of ink onto the glass. Push the brayer over the glass until it is evenly covered with ink.

4. Roll the brayer over the shape on the block.

5. Press the block down firmly on the paper you are printing.

6. As soon as you finish printing—before the ink hardens—clean brayer, block, pane of glass, and your hands.

236

DRAWING AND PAINTING

A drawing can say many things. It can tell the fun of a trip, hike, cookout, or the excitement of a holiday party. You can express ideas, too. Draw what the Girl Scout Laws mean to you. Draw what makes you think of being cheerful, friendly, courteous.

You can make many different colors by mixing tempera paints. Add white to a color and see what happens. Mix two colors, three colors. Mix small amounts of paint, in small paper cups or foil containers. For a sharp contrast in your picture, use touches of black in your painting. For a sparkling effect, let touches of white paper show through. Do not worry if you make a mistake, paint right over it.

When you finish painting, clean your brushes with water so they will be ready to use the next time.

Experiment with colored chalks. Put one color on top of another. Put a color on heavily, then rub to shade it. Try dipping the chalk in water or drawing on dampened paper. Try drawing with charcoal from a campfire. Spray a chalk drawing lightly when you are finished so it will not smear. The spray is called a "fixative" or plastic spray and is sold in art supply stores.

Mount your drawings and paintings on white or colored sheets of stiff paper. This will show off your paintings.

One patrol or even the entire troop can paint a picture at the same time by making a mural on sheets of long paper. Paint a mural to use for the background for a troop play.

PICTURES WITH YARN

Making a picture with yarn and fabric is fun, too. Cut designs
from different kinds of material and fasten the designs onto
a background of cloth with colorful yarn or embroidery floss.
You can add buttons and tape, felt or lace for decoration. A
heavy cloth is best for your background—burlap, monks
cloth, or hopsacking. While you work, hold the material in
place with a small dab of rubber cement.

You do not need to know special stitches. Use your needle in
your own way to make short or long stitches. Cross the
stitches or make them straight. Make up your own designs
with them.

If you want to use embroidery stitches, ask your mother or
your sewing teacher to show you one or two of these: Cross
stitch, French knot, blanket or buttonhole stitch, couching,
satin stitch, running stitch. When you know embroidery
stitches, you can make a sampler. Design your own sampler
to show one of your hobbies, your house, your pet, your
favorite poem.

238

COLLAGE

You can make a wonderful picture with just scraps of material or paper and odds and ends.

Collect a box full of different kinds of paper and fabric scraps —tissue, wallpaper samples, printed paper, candy papers, foil, cellophane in colors, velvets, cotton, denim, fur bits.

Collect pieces of ribbon, yarn, rickrack, some buttons, paper clips, pieces of sponge, pipe cleaners.

Choose papers, fabrics, and objects that you like together. Glue or staple these to a background of cardboard or heavy paper.

CLAY

Roll, bend, twist, shape, pat clay any way you like. You can work with clay and then use it again and again to make new figures and shapes. Sometimes you might find clay along a creek bank. Sometimes you buy it.

There are many different colors in natural clay—white, gray, red—depending on where you live. There are many clay substitutes, which are fun to model. But only real clay can be baked and kept a long time. Try to find someone who can show you how to prepare clay and glaze it and fire it in a kiln.

To make a figure of clay:

1. Make balls and coils of clay for the head, legs, and body by rolling the clay between the palms of your hands. Keep forms large enough to work with easily.

2. Put these forms together in a shape you like. To make the pieces of clay stick together, use "slip." Make slip by adding water to powdered clay until it is like thick cream. Dip the pieces you want to join into the slip, then press them together firmly.

3. Bend or straighten legs and body to make the figure sit up or lie down. Tilt or turn the head.

4. Add little pieces of clay for the nose, ears, hair. For special effects, scratch or scrape the clay with a fork, knife, or twig.

PAPIER MÂCHÉ

Puppet heads, masks, figures of animals and people, holiday ornaments are some things you can make with papier mâché.

You need: Newspapers, string, white paste, poster paints.

To make an animal of papier mâché:

1. Roll several sheets of newspaper toward the fold. To make your figure stronger, insert a piece of wire in the newspaper roll.

2. Tie string around each end of the roll and also around the middle.

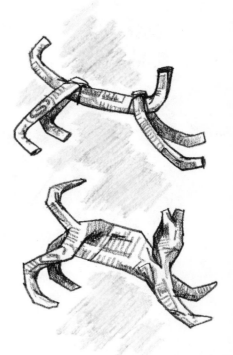

3. Bend and tie rolls together to make animals.

4. Paste on ears or a tail or mane.

5. Tear newspaper into small strips and squares.

6. Paste strips and small squares of newspaper over the figure. Overlap the strips.

7. Let your figure dry. Paint it.

241

KITES

All over the world children fly kites—box kites and fish kites, diamond kites and star kites. Make a kite for yourself or for a friend. Invite another troop or your father to make and fly kites with you. Fly your kite safely—away from electric wires and never in the rain.

You need: Two sticks, two or three feet long and ¼ to ⅜ inches wide; tissue or wrapping paper to cover kite; cord; glue or rubber cement; plastic tape; strip of cloth; ribbons and bows for the tail.

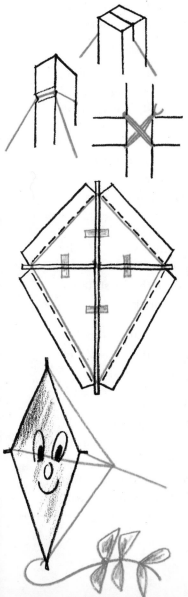

1. Take sticks and notch with knife or make a split with a coping saw in each of the ends to hold the string around the kite.

2. Glue cross sticks. Tie with cord.

3. String the cord around the sticks to outline the kite. Tie cord around notches or slip it into slits.

4. Tape sticks on kite paper and draw outline around the string.

5. Cut paper so it is two inches bigger than outline of kite. Fold margin of paper over the string, and glue.

6. Decorate your kite by painting it or by pasting on pieces of colored paper.

7. Tie a piece of cord to each of the four corners and knot the cords together. This makes a "bridle." Experiment to find the best place to tie the long cord to the bridle.

8. Add a tail of cloth to balance the kite. Add ribbons or paper bows to make it look gay. On windy days you will need a heavier tail than on other days.

A TOY VILLAGE

Scrap lumber from a lumber yard is just right for making an entire village. Ask for a variety of scraps and sizes.

You need these tools: A coping saw to cut curves and notches; a vise or clamp to hold the wood while you saw; a knife to whittle away small pieces and give special shapes to your village.

You need these materials: Sandpaper, coarse and fine; wood glue; poster paints; paste wax; two brushes—a flat brush for covering large areas and a small, fine-pointed brush for painting small details.

The shapes of the wood will help you decide on the size and kind of village to build. Look at pictures to get ideas. Build a modern city block or a city of tomorrow. Build a farm or ranch, airport or a medieval castle.

Saw, whittle, and glue the wood together until you have the shape you want. You may want to carve a special door or an arch with your knife. Sand the wood smooth. First use a coarse grade of sandpaper, then use fine sandpaper.

Paint your village carefully. Outline areas for different colors with pencil. You may paint just a door or roof top. When the paint is dry, rub on paste wax and polish gently.

You can make wooden animals, people, or trees for your village. Draw each figure on paper, then trace it on the wood. Saw around the outline with a coping saw. Whittle away small pieces to give your figure the shape you want. You may either leave knife marks showing or sand your figure smooth. If you paint it, sand it first. Rub your figure with paste wax and polish gently.

TOYS

Many things described in this chapter would make good toys and gifts. Make them as a service project or give them as gifts to your family and friends.

Before you plan a service project, find out what kind of toys are needed. Find out if certain materials should be used. Small children and babies often chew toys, drop them, and throw them. They may swallow small parts, so be sure toys have none. Edges should be smooth. Do not use staples or wires to hold parts together. Do not use paint with a lead base.

Set up a toy workshop at your troop meeting. Make jump ropes with colored whippings at the ends, games and puzzles, kites or puppets, stuffed animals or a doll house complete with furniture, a toy village. Make toys you would like to receive.

WEAVING

There are many kinds of weaving. Weaving on a square frame is one kind you probably know. Weaving on a tee dee loom, an Indian type, is another kind. On a tee dee loom you can weave a belt or headband or tie.

To make a belt on a tee dee loom:

You need: Ten ice cream sticks or tongue depressors, wood glue, cord, wood stick about one inch thick and six inches long; tape or rope long enough to fit around your waist; newspaper; cardboard; hand drill; knife or coping saw; carpet warp or string for warp threads; candlewicking or thick yarn scraps for woof threads.

To make the loom:

1. Drill a small hole in the center of six sticks. Warp threads go through these holes.

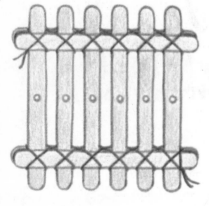

heddle

2. Take two more sticks and place them, on a piece of newspaper, in position for cross pieces of the heddle as in the picture.

3. Spread glue on the two cross pieces. Place the six sticks with holes across the two cross pieces as in the picture. Leave enough space between the sticks for a warp thread to pass between the sticks. Take the last two sticks and glue them across the six sticks, facing the first two cross sticks. Now you have a heddle. Put something heavy on it and let it dry.

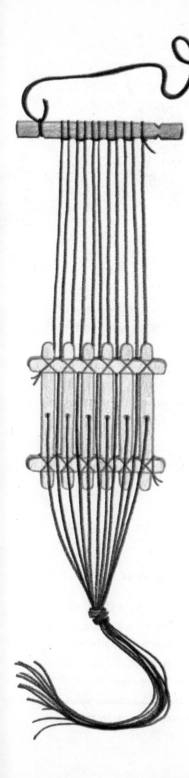

4. When the glue is dry, tie the sticks in place with the cord.

5. Take the six-inch stick and whittle a notch around it near each end. Tie one end of the tape or rope around one notch. Put the stick in front of your stomach and bring the tape around in back of you and in front. Make a loop in this end to slip in the other notch.

6. Cut warp threads from carpet warp or string. Cut one warp thread the length of your belt plus 18 inches. Cut five more warp threads twice as long as the first one.

7. Tie the first warp thread to the six-inch stick with a square knot. Fold the other warp threads in half. Take each folded thread and wrap the fold loop around the stick. Pull both ends through the loop.

8. Thread the first warp thread through the hole in the first stick of the heddle. Pass the second warp thread between the first and second stick. Thread the third warp through the hole in the second stick. Continue in this way until all eleven warps are threaded. Tie all the ends together with an overhand knot.

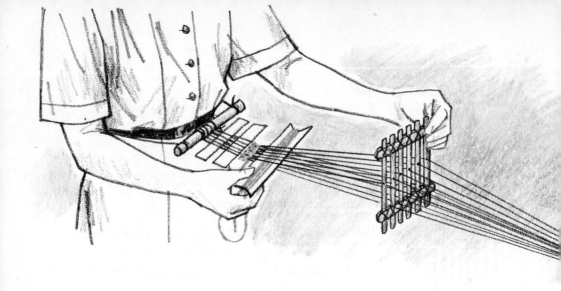

9. Cut a shuttle out of cardboard about one inch wide and longer than the heddle is wide. Notch the ends of the shuttle. Wind the thick woof thread around the shuttle. If you want different colors on your belt, use several different colored woof threads, each on its own shuttle.

10. Cut two strips of cardboard ½ inch wide and as long as the heddle.

To weave:

1. Fasten the knot of warps to a chair, hook, or tree.

2. Fasten the tape around your waist.

3. Start weaving close to your body. First weave in the two pieces of cardboard: Raise the heddle. The warp threads will form an opening called a "shed." Put one of the cardboard strips in the shed. Lower the heddle. This will make a second shed. Put the second cardboard strip in there.

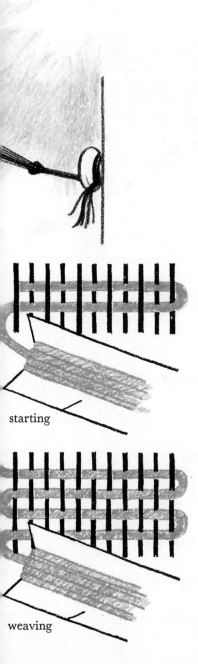

starting

weaving

4. Start the yarn: Raise the heddle with your left hand and pass the shuttle through, from the right to the left, with your right hand. The yarn will lay between the warps. Shift the heddle to your right hand and with your left hand pass the shuttle around the last warp thread. With the heddle still raised, pass the shuttle back, from left to right. The yarn comes back between the same warps and is anchored. Every time you start a new color or put more yarn on your shuttle, start and finish your yarn this way.

5. Weave: Drop the heddle and pass the shuttle through, from right to left, from your right hand to your left hand. Raise the heddle with your right hand and pass the shuttle back with your left hand. Continue to do this for the length of your belt. After you weave five or six inches, wrap the weaving around the stick at your waist so you can weave easily. Do not pull your weaving too tight. Keep the edges straight and even.

6. Finish: Cut the ends of the warp threads tied to the stick. Remove the cardboard strips and knot the warp threads together with a square knot. Pull the knot up tight against the weaving to keep it from unraveling. Cut and knot the other end the same way.

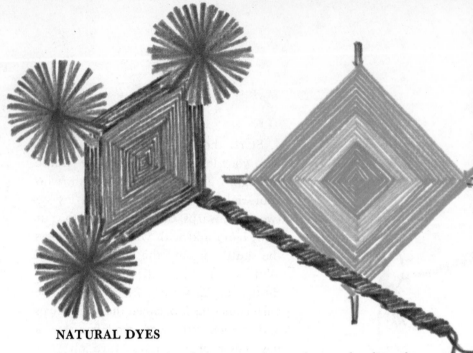

NATURAL DYES

Berries, stems, barks, flowers can be used to make dyes that will color cloth or yarn. Use ripe berries, flowers and leaves at full bloom, bark collected in spring or early summer, roots collected in early fall.

Make the dye

1. Chop plants into small pieces and cover with water. Soak overnight.

2. Boil for an hour or more, until color is much deeper than color you want.

3. Strain, to remove all pieces of plants.

Prepare materials to be dyed

1. Wash and rinse cloth in soap and water.

2. Add one ounce of alum to a gallon of water. Also add ¼ ounce of washing soda if cloth is made of a vegetable fiber—cotton, linen, or rayon. If cloth is made of an animal fiber—silk or wool—add ¼ ounce cream of tartar.

3. Put cloth in this solution and boil for an hour. Rinse and dry.

250

Dye the material

1. Use a kettle large enough to hold the dye and cloth to be dyed—an enamel kettle is good. Add enough water that the dye will cover the cloth.

2. Bring liquid to a boil and add cloth. Stir with a wooden stick.

3. Lift the cloth on the stick so that you can see light through it. The color will be close to the color your cloth will be when it dries. You may have to boil the cloth in the dye from a half an hour to an hour to get it the shade you want.

4. "Set" the dye so it will not wash out. Add ½ cup of vinegar or one tablespoon of salt to the liquid in the kettle. Boil for fifteen minutes.

5. Remove the cloth from the dye. Rinse in cool water. Hang in the shade to dry.

These plants make these colors.

Goldenrod stalk and flowers	Yellow
Sumac leaves	Yellow brown
Onion skins	Red or yellow
Beets	Red violet
Dandelion roots	Magenta
Rhubarb leaves	Light green
Spinach leaves	Green
Blackberries	Blue
Sunflower seeds	Blue
Hickory bark	Brown
Walnut hulls	Brown

CEREMONIES
AND
CELEBRATIONS

Girl Scouts have many ceremonies. They say their Promise in the glow of candlelight. They make wishes round a campfire on a starry night. They hold a Scouts' Own at the close of day. They celebrate Girl Scout birthdays in a special way.

Sometimes your own troop or camp unit has a ceremony just for itself. Other times you will decide to invite another troop or parents or friends to attend.

When you have guests, explain what the occasion is, so they can share the way you feel about it. If you want guests to stand or sing during any part, give them directions as you go along. Decide ahead of time how you will start your ceremony and who will announce or lead each part.

253

FLAG OR "COLOR" CEREMONY

We honor our country's flag at a flag ceremony and show that we are proud to be citizens of the United States of America. Sometimes your troop will open or close a meeting with a flag ceremony. Sometimes it will be part of longer ceremonies or celebrations in this chapter.

Stand straight and tall, with your hands at your sides, during a flag ceremony. You will be told when to do what by the Scout-in-charge.

The color guard is a guard of honor for the flag. It is made up of a color bearer and color guards.

The color bearer is the person who carries the flag, either on a staff or folded if it is to be raised or lowered on a flag-pole. If there is going to be more than one flag, there is a color bearer for each flag. The color bearer may wear a red sash over her right shoulder in the same position as the badge sash. It ties in a square knot on the left side of her waist.

Two or more color guards stand on each side of the bearer and see that the flag does not touch the ground. Guards may also wear red sashes. Their sashes go around the waist and tie in a square knot on the left.

Girl Scouts usually assemble in a horseshoe formation for a flag ceremony. The Scout-in-charge of the ceremony stands at one end of the horseshoe.

The Scout-in-charge says, "Color guard, advance." The color guard steps back out of the horseshoe and walks to the flag.

Before the color bearer picks up the flag of the United States of America, the entire color guard lines up and faces the flag. The color bearer gives a quiet command. "Salute." She and the guards place their hands over their hearts for a second. Then the bearer picks up the flag. If the flagstaff needs to be unscrewed or loosened, one of the guards does this. If other flags are being used in the ceremony, their bearers pick them up *after* the flag of the United States of America has been picked up but they do not salute those flags.

The color guard then wheels to the right, marches to the open part of the horseshoe, and faces the troop. During the rest of the ceremony, the color guard stands silently at attention.

The Scout-in-charge announces the next part of the ceremony. Choose different songs and things to say or read for this part of the ceremony—patriotic songs, poems, words written by a troop member. Make every ceremony different. Give each one a special meaning. Make a patrol collection of things you would like to read or say at a flag ceremony so you will be prepared whenever you are asked to present one.

At the end of the ceremony, the Scout-in-charge says, "Color guard, post the colors." The color guard wheels to the right and marches back to the flag stand. The flag of our country is posted *after* all other flags. After the color bearer places the flag in the holder, the color guard salutes the flag. Then they return to their place in the horseshoe.

A group planning a flag ceremony might use these notes.

Who will carry the flag?——————————————

Who will be the guards?——————————————

Who will give directions for the ceremony?——————

What song shall we sing?——————————————

   Who will start the song?——————————————

Do we want a poem, a quotation?——————————

   Who will say it?——————————————

After the Pledge of Allegiance,
shall we say the Girl Scout Promise and Laws?—————

In what order shall we do these things?——————

SALUTING THE FLAG

Salute the flag of the United States of America by placing
your right hand over your heart:

* When you give the Pledge of Allegiance.

* The moment the flag passes in front of you in a parade.

* From the moment a flag starts being raised up a pole
  until the moment it reaches the top.

* From the moment a flag starts to be lowered on a pole until
  both clasps are in the hands of the color bearer.

* When the flag is present and "The Star-Spangled Banner"
  is played. If you sing, stand at attention.

When other flags are presented, do not salute.

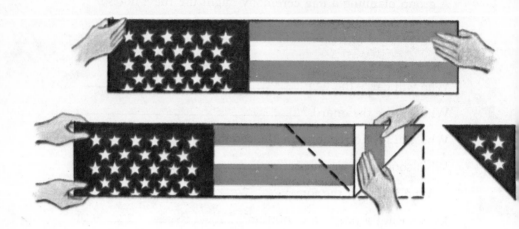

DISPLAYING THE FLAG

Public Law 829 tells civilians how to display and use the flag of the United States of America. Follow this code when flying the flag in your yard or meeting place, at camp.

The flag should be displayed only from sunrise to sunset. It should be raised quickly and lowered slowly. It should not be displayed in bad weather.

When flags of two or more nations are displayed, they must be flown from separate poles of the same height. The flags should be the same size.

When the American flag is hung against a wall, the blue field should be uppermost and to the flag's own right. When hung across a street, the flag's blue field must be north or east.

The flag should never be used as a drapery or cover except at a funeral. No object should ever be placed on the flag. It should not be allowed to touch the floor or ground.

An old flag should be destroyed, preferably by burning.

CANDLELIGHT CEREMONY WITH THE PROMISE AND LAW

When girls join your troop or you have a Court of Awards or Scouts' Own, you can have a candle lighting ceremony with the Promise and Law. Candle lighting and the Promise and Law can be a part of many ceremonies.

In this ceremony the troop stands in a horseshoe with a table at the open end. On the table there are three large candles and ten smaller candles.

The leader or a troop member explains that the three candles stand for the three parts of the Girl Scout Promise. She lights the three candles as the troop repeats the Promise together. Then troop members light the ten candles and say each of the ten parts of the Girl Scout Law.

A good song for this ceremony is "Whene'er You Make a Promise" on page 192.

INVESTITURE AND REDEDICATION CEREMONIES

At an Investiture ceremony, a new girl makes her Girl Scout Promise, receives her pin, and becomes a member of the Girl Scouts. She is a Junior Girl Scout.

At a Rededication ceremony, following a fly-up ceremony, a Brownie Girl Scout makes her Girl Scout Promise, receives her pin, and becomes a Junior Girl Scout.

Many troops have a flag ceremony or a candlelight ceremony as part of Investiture or Rededication. When all the candles have been lighted, the leader asks the new girls if they are ready to make their Promise. They give the Girl Scout sign and make their Promise. The leader pins the Girl Scout pin and the World Association pin on them and welcomes them with the Girl Scout handshake.

INSTALLATION OF PATROL LEADERS

When new patrol leaders begin to serve a troop, the troop has a ceremony in which they are given their patrol leader cords. A patrol leader wears a cord on her left shoulder as a sign of her office. The cord has two gold circles which represent the two circles of people the patrol leader serves— her own patrol and the whole troop.

At the beginning of the ceremony the troop leader announces the purpose of the ceremony and asks that the new patrol leader be presented to the troop. If each patrol elected its own leader, one member of each patrol presents her new leader. If the entire troop elected the patrol leaders, the previous patrol leaders bring the new leaders forward.

Then the troop leader talks to the patrol leaders about the meaning of the cords they will wear. She asks them if they will do their best to live up to the patrols' trust. She asks the patrol members if they will do their best to be loyal and helpful to their patrol leader.

Next, the girls who are presenting the patrol leaders, pin the cords on the new leaders and give them the Girl Scout handshake. The new patrol leaders step back into the troop circle.

The troop leader reminds the patrol leaders that the second circle in the cord is a symbol of the entire troop they serve at the Court of Honor.

Then the troop may make a friendship circle and sing a song.

JULIETTE LOW'S BIRTHDAY—October 31

Juliette Low was born on Halloween. She loved to dress up and go to parties. To celebrate her birthday, you can dress up as things or people who lived when she did.

Daisy Low wished that girls from many different countries would be friends. The Juliette Low World Friendship Fund (see page 29) is a way you can help that wish come true. If a Senior Girl Scout in your council has met girls from other countries, invite her to your troop meeting to tell you about them.

On pages 164-165 there is a wide game about Juliette Low.

TROOP BIRTHDAY

Your troop's birthday is the day you renew your Girl Scout membership for the coming year. Each troop member has paid her dollar membership dues, and on your troop birthday your leader gives each girl her registration card. This card shows that you belong to the Girl Scout movement in the United States of America for the coming year. When every girl has her card, the whole troop might say the Girl Scout Promise together.

Each girl who has been a Girl Scout for the past year receives a membership star. People "wish upon a star" and also make wishes when they blow out birthday candles, so why not make wishes on your troop's birthday? Wish for something you want your troop to do next year. If you are meeting around a campfire, you can each make a wish as you lay a stick on the fire. Or make your wishes on real stars

GIRL SCOUT BIRTHDAY AND GIRL SCOUT WEEK

The first troop of Girl Scouts in the United States met on March 12, 1912 and that is the Girl Scout Birthday. Girl Scouts call the week of March 12 "Girl Scout Week."

During Girl Scout Week, troops often celebrate by showing their town some of the things Girl Scouts do. They do a good turn or service project.

Your troop could cut forsythia or other flowering shrubs before March 12. Put the cuttings in water so they will flower. Then give them to someone or put them where people will enjoy them during Girl Scout Week. Make a card for the flowers saying that the Girl Scouts are celebrating their Birthday.

Troops have art shows or displays at a public library, in store windows. They serenade neighborhood friends. They often attend religious services in uniform during Girl Scout Week.

Lay the membership stars in a circle around the cake so that after the candles are blown out, each girl can pick up a star and pin it on the girl standing next to her.

THINKING DAY—February 22

Girl Scouts and Girl Guides all over the world celebrate Thinking Day. They link thoughts around the earth that all people shall be friends. They have celebrations and get together with other troops. They do this on February 22 because that is the birthday of Lord and Lady Baden-Powell.

Thinking Day starts in New Zealand where the dawn of the new day first touches land. Guides in New Zealand rise before daylight and go to the top of a mountain. When they see the first light, they start the chain of thoughts that will circle the globe with the sun on Thinking Day.

In Iceland, Guides from many troops meet together. Ten Guides stand up in front, each holding a candle. The candles are lighted and placed in holders as everyone says the Laws together. Then everyone says, "Every Guide is a good friend and sister to every other Guide." The Guides shake hands with each other, using the Girl Scout handshake, and they sing a song of friendship.

Netherlands Guides gather early in the morning to raise the World Association flag and renew their Promise. Then they

264

may say, "I am a link in the golden chain of World Scouting and I must keep my link strong and bright."

All over the world Girl Guides and Scouts send greetings to each other with Thinking Day cards. You could make and send Thinking Day friendship cards to Girl Scouts you met at camp or Scouts right in your own town. Thinking Day is a time to make new friends as well as to remember old friends. Greet friends with words in another language (page 177). Your troop can get together with another troop, or several troops, for a song fest, a folk dance or games party. Hold a Scouts' Own on friendship. Include a story, poems, or songs about friendship.

At a candlelight ceremony, your troop may repeat the Girl Scout Promise as other Girl Scouts and Girl Guides around the world do. You may sing a song or say a Law in another language. In addition to the thirteen candles for the Promise and the ten parts of the Law, you might light a candle for the World Association and for your motto. Each girl could light a candle for one of the things that Thinking Day means to her.

265

SCOUTS' OWN

A Scouts' Own is a ceremony expressing the spirit of Girl Scouting. A Scouts' Own is not a religious service and does not take the place of going to church or synagogue.

When and where. A Scouts' Own can be held any time, indoors or outdoors, as part of a troop meeting or a camping trip. Your troop may have a Scouts' Own on Thinking Day, New Year's Day, your troop's birthday, or national holidays. You can open or close a troop meeting or a day at camp with a Scouts' Own. Have it around a campfire, at sunrise or sunset.

It is a Girl Scout custom to assemble and walk quietly to the place where the Scouts' Own is to be held and to leave quietly after it is over.

Choose a place you especially like—one with a pretty view, by a stream or pond, under a tree, a spot where you can see the sky. Indoors, choose a symbol—a picture or flag or leaves—that represents the theme of your Scouts' Own.

How to plan a Scouts' Own. A small group, such as one patrol or the Court of Honor, usually plans a Scouts' Own with the help of their troop leader.

1. First choose a theme. Then make a list of different ways you can tell or show the theme.

2. From your list choose one idea to open the Scouts' Own. Select the other ideas you want to include—one or two or half a dozen. Arrange them in an order you like. Decide how to end the Scouts' Own.

3. Decide who will perform or lead each part and who will lead the girls to the place for the ceremony and back again.

The Girl Scout Law or a part of it might be the theme for your Scouts' Own. Your theme might be our country, its different peoples, your part as a citizen. Your theme might be the forests and rivers and mountains of our country. Your theme might be the spirit of a special occasion such as Thanksgiving or the first day of spring.

Express your theme in one or more of these ways:

* Songs for everyone to sing

* Music played by one or two girls

* Shadow play scene

* Poems or quotations

* Words a troop member writes for the Scouts' Own

* Choral reading

* Stories and legends

* Girl Scout Promise, Girl Scout Law

* Pledge of Allegiance

* Conservation Pledge

* Thoughts about what the theme means to her spoken by each Scout. If several troops are having a Scouts' Own together, each troop could contribute a thought.

SYMBOLS

Standing in New York harbor where everyone can see is the Statue of Liberty, symbol of the free. There are many other symbols anywhere you look—on stamps and coins and even in the pages of this book. Your Girl Scout pin, your country's flag are symbols too, you know. Look around and you will find symbols everywhere you go.

A symbol is a sign that stands for something very important, an idea or a belief. A symbol may be an animal or a person, a special place or something you do. A symbol may stand for courage and truth, freedom and loyalty and love. Girl Scout badges are symbols of skills you have and readiness to help. The song "The Star-Spangled Banner" is a symbol of our country's fight for freedom. Flowers are symbols, too. Which flower is your state flower? Every religion has its own symbols. What religious symbols do you know?

Words can be symbols. Look on a penny and you will see the Latin words *E pluribus unum*. Those words mean "out of the many, one" and to citizens of the United States of America that symbolizes "many states, one nation." On your penny you will also see the motto "In God we trust."

269

People can be symbols, too. Uncle Sam, with his long beard, dressed in stars and stripes, stands for the United States of America to us and to the people in other countries. Paul Bunyan, the giant logger, is a symbol in folk stories of the strong men who helped build our country.

You can tell the story or meaning of a symbol as a part of a Scouts' Own, flag ceremony, opening or closing of a meeting. At a folk legend party you can dress up and act out folk stories.

The Girl Scout Pin

Your Girl Scout pin is a symbol of the Girl Scout Promise you make and the three parts of that Promise. You read about this on page 23. The initials "G.S." on the pin stand for Girl Scouts, of course.

The Great Seal of
the United States of Ame**r**

The shield and eagle are parts of the Great Seal of the United States of America. On the shield are thirteen stripes which represent the thirteen original states. The bar across the top stands for the United States Congress uniting all the states.

The eagle is a symbol of strength and victory. He is facing right, a symbol of honor. He holds arrows—a symbol of power—and an olive branch—a symbol of peace.

270

1775

1777

1795

Our Flag

Flags of red and white stripes were a symbol of bravery and freedom before our country became independent. The pilgrims brought a flag of red and white stripes with them when they came to America.

On June 14, 1777 it was decreed that our flag "be thirteen stripes, alternate red and white; that the union be thirteen stars, white in a blue field, representing a new constellation." Many years later John Quincy Adams, sixth President of the United States, wrote that the people who helped write the Constitution hoped our country might be a symbol of peace in the world. They hoped the stars in the flag could be like the stars in the constellation Lyra, named for the lyre, a symbol of harmony and peace.

Whenever a new state joins the United States a new star is added to the flag. The fiftieth star was added just a few years ago when Hawaii became a state in 1960. When did a star for your state become part of the flag? The thirteen stripes on the flag never change. They stand for the first thirteen states to form our nation. They stand for freedom and courage and they always will.

NATURE

Hurry, hurry, hurry to the world's greatest show. Hurry, hurry to your seat in the very first row! You don't need a ticket. Just use your eyes, and see nature's changes in the land, the seas, the skies. One day you'll spy flowers blooming, bright and sweet, to make a glorious springtime carpet at your feet. Then, when winter's cold winds begin to blow,

you'll see nature's creatures prepare for snow. There are changes every month, every week, every day. Look around you at the wonders of nature's way. You'll see moths where there were cocoons before. You'll see nuts ripen, leaves fall —and more and more and more! Use your eyes, your ears, your touch when you explore. For the world's greatest show is right outside your door.

273

duck

oriole

flamingo

bluebird

274

goldfinch

parrot

redwinged blackbird

Birds

A good time to watch birds is when they
feed, especially just before dusk or early
in the morning. But be quick. They sit
still for only a few minutes.

Feathers. How many different colors are there in the bird's feathers? Mother birds usually have soft colors so they are hard to see when they sit on their nests. Their colors protect them. Male birds have bright colored feathers and are easier to see.

Birds are the only animals with feathers. When you find a feather, look at it with a magnifying glass. The edge of the feather sticks together and keeps the rain from coming through. On cold days birds fluff their feathers to keep warm, just as you wear thick, fluffy winter clothes. The fluffed feathers keep warm air close to the bird's body.

Tail. What shape is the bird's tail? Short? Long? Square at the tip? Rounded? Forked? A bird's tail helps it to steer as it flies. Watch a bird "land." It spreads its tail feathers and uses its tail as a brake to slow itself down. Its wings help it stop, too. A bird that can perch on the trunk of a tree—a woodpecker, for instance—uses its tail as a brace.

Head. Is the top of the bird's head smooth, or does it have a tuft, or crest of feathers?

Nests. Each type of bird builds a different kind of nest. Never move a nest unless it is winter or late fall and the bird is finished using it as a home for its young family. Some birds build nests in branches, others in grass or hollow trees or corners of buildings.

Bill. The shape of a bird's bill tells you the kind of food it eats. Short, sturdy bills are good for cracking seeds. Sharp, slender bills can pick insects from cracks in trees. Curved bills are good for tearing meat. A hummingbird can reach nectar in flowers with his long pointed bill. Some birds use their bills to catch fish.

Feet and Legs. Most birds have three toes in front and one toe in back. They can grasp twigs and sit on wires. The woodpecker has two toes in front and two in back. With these toes he can cling to the trunk of a tree. Webfeet are good for swimming. Long legs are good for wading to look for fish.

Calls. Be very quiet at dusk, or early morning, and listen. Some birds sing lovely songs. Other birds seem to say things —"Whippoorwill"—"Peter"—"Caw-caw." Some birds have cheerful calls. Sometimes birds call warnings.

Season. You see some birds year round. Other birds stay only for a season, or pass through your part of the country on the way north or south. When migrating, small birds usually travel at night, large birds during the day.

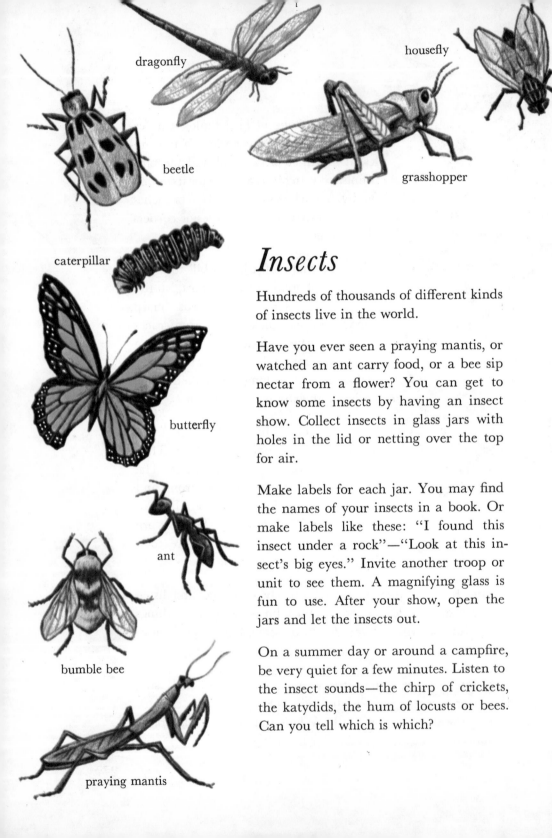

dragonfly

housefly

beetle

grasshopper

caterpillar

butterfly

ant

bumble bee

praying mantis

Insects

Hundreds of thousands of different kinds of insects live in the world.

Have you ever seen a praying mantis, or watched an ant carry food, or a bee sip nectar from a flower? You can get to know some insects by having an insect show. Collect insects in glass jars with holes in the lid or netting over the top for air.

Make labels for each jar. You may find the names of your insects in a book. Or make labels like these: "I found this insect under a rock"—"Look at this insect's big eyes." Invite another troop or unit to see them. A magnifying glass is fun to use. After your show, open the jars and let the insects out.

On a summer day or around a campfire, be very quiet for a few minutes. Listen to the insect sounds—the chirp of crickets, the katydids, the hum of locusts or bees. Can you tell which is which?

toad

salamander

bullfrog

Amphibians

Frogs, toads, and salamanders are amphibians. They live part of their lives in the water, part on land. Amphibian means living in two places.

Frogs and toads lay eggs in water, salamanders in moist places. The eggs hatch into tadpoles. Tadpoles live in water. They have no legs and breathe through gills. Gradually legs appear. The gills disappear and lungs develop. Then they can live on land.

Toads are found mostly on land. You may find a toad out looking for food in a garden or in the woods, sometimes in a hole he has dug with his hind legs. A toad's skin looks nubbly.

Frogs live in and out of water. Listen for them on spring or summer evenings. Spring peepers or tree frogs make a high-pitched peep. Bull frogs make a low croak. Toads sing, too. To make a noise, a frog or toad fills his throat with air. It swells like a balloon. Then the air goes back and forth over his vocal chords and out comes music. "Frog Round" in the *Girl Scout Pocket Songbook* has peeps and croaks in it.

Look for salamanders after a rain, in damp, woody places.

279

Reptiles

Snakes, turtles, lizards, crocodiles, and alligators are reptiles. You may have to go to a zoo to see some of these reptiles. Others you can see in gardens or fields or woods. All reptiles have scales. Dinosaurs were reptiles. Dinosaur means "terrible lizard."

A snake feels soft and wiggly. If you hold one, you can feel its muscles move. Snakes help man by eating mice and insects. There are only a few poisonous snakes which you should learn to recognize and avoid if they live in your part of the country.

Snakes cannot hear. They feel vibrations on the ground and know a person or animal is coming. The snake's tongue flicks in and out and helps guide it in its continuing search for food. A snake sheds its skin as it grows. You might find such a skin someday. Notice the part that came off over the eyes.

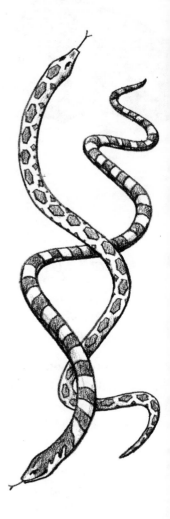

Turtles have shells. Some kinds of turtles can pull head, feet, and tail inside the shell to protect themselves. These are called box turtles. If you have ever watched a turtle's neck, you know why high-necked sweaters are called "turtle neck."

Mammals

Do you know how elephants, whales, mice, cows, squirrels, giraffes, and bats are alike? They are alike in that they are all mammals, which means their babies are nursed by the mother. You are a mammal too. It is true that they are all animals, but insects and fish and birds and reptiles are also part of the animal kingdom. A mammal is a special kind of an animal.

Pets

What kind of pet do you have? Many people choose cats, dogs, birds, fish, or turtles as pets. Some people choose more unusual pets—monkeys, parrots, or wild animals such as chipmunks or raccoons. All pets need kindness and care. They need the proper food and water. They need clean places to rest and live. And they need exercise.

dog

rabbit

raccoon

bear

Tracks— Who Walked Here?

Most animals are timid and have learned to hide themselves well. But if you look closely, you will find clues that they have passed by.

Look for tracks along the edges of water, where the animals come to drink. Look on a desert, or in snow. Look on a farm for tracks of animals that live on the farm. Look at the tracks your pet makes after he walks through a puddle.

Animals that hop or walk: Dogs leave claw marks when they walk. Cats can pull their claws in.

Animals that bound: You can tell from the tracks of a rabbit how far it jumps. Animals that bound put their hind legs ahead of their front legs.

Heel and toe walkers: Some animals walk on both their heels and toes just as people do. Have you ever watched a raccoon or bear walk?

SKETCHING TRACKS

You can make sketches of animal tracks you find in dust or snow or damp earth.

If you cannot find tracks, put bits of fruit or vegetable, berries, raw meat, seeds, down in the center of a dusty or snowy or moist place. Smooth the dust. The animals will come for the food during the night. If there are no animal tracks the next morning, try another kind of food.

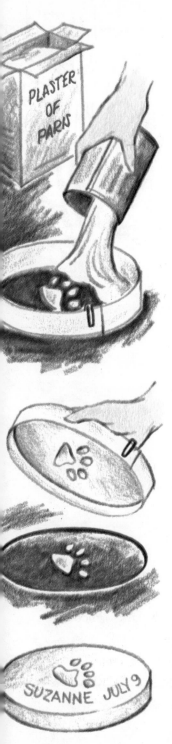

MAKING PLASTER CASTS

The best tracks for casting are found in mud. Get your pet's track in a pan of moist dirt or take these casting supplies with you on a hike.

You need: Plaster of Paris for casts, water, a strip of cardboard one and a half inches wide, paper clip, empty tin can, brush, sponge, stick for stirring.

1. Brush away all twigs, small stones, or dirt on the ground around the tracks. Sponge up any water in the tracks.

2. Surround tracks with strip of cardboard. Fasten in place with paper clip. Push cardboard halfway down in mud.

3. Put about a cupful of water in the can. Pour dry plaster slowly into water, stirring with stick until mixture is thick and smooth as pancake batter. Pour plaster *slowly* over tracks, inside cardboard form, from one end to the other. This way the plaster has time to push the air out and no air bubbles are left in the cast.

4. In fifteen minutes the plaster will harden enough for you to pick up the cast. While the cast is still damp, scratch the name of the animal, the date you found the tracks, and your initials on the back of it. After two days you can remove the cardboard and scrape away the mud.

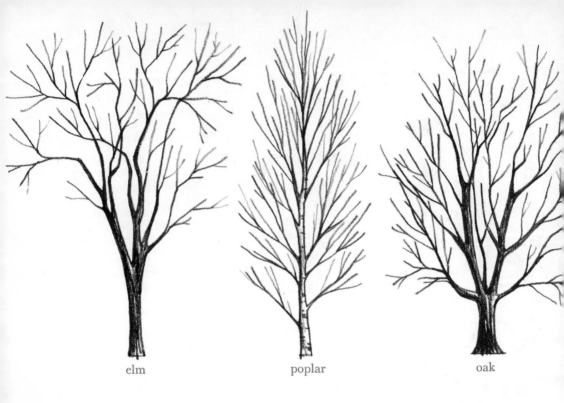

elm   poplar   oak

Trees

TREE GAME

See how sharp your eyes are. Here are tips on how to look at trees. Play this game on a hike with your troop or in the yard of your meeting place or at camp or as you walk home from school. Find trees like these:

☐ A tree with branches that spread out, like a fan—that bend toward the earth— that point to the sky—that reach out.

☐ A tree with a tall, straight trunk, like a flagpole.

☐ A tree with gray bark—black bark—rough bark—smooth bark—peeling bark—white bark—greenish bark.

☐ A tree that has been injured. What caused the injury?

☐ A tree whose leaves are pointed—rounded—saw-toothed—smooth-edged—needlelike.

284

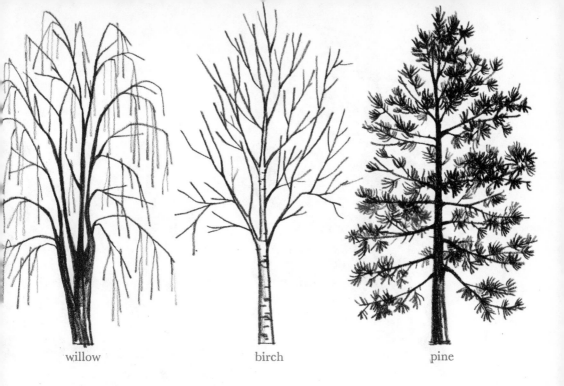

willow   birch   pine

☐ A tree that has food for animals, for birds, for people.

☐ A tree that has a home for birds, for animals.

☐ Trees that have flowers or seeds or buds.

You can sketch tree shapes, especially in winter. See if others can recognize the trees from your sketches.

LEAVES OF TREES

In the spring and summer, leaves help you to tell trees apart. Most trees in this country are either broad-leaved trees or conifers. Most broad-leaved trees shed their leaves when the weather turns cold, although some keep their leaves all year round, the live oak for instance. Conifers have cones and long thin leaves called needles. Most conifers are known as evergreens because they keep their needles all year long. Some conifers lose their needles in the fall, the larch for instance. Pine, spruce, and cedar are evergreens you may know.

285

red maple

white oak

black locust

286

dogwoo

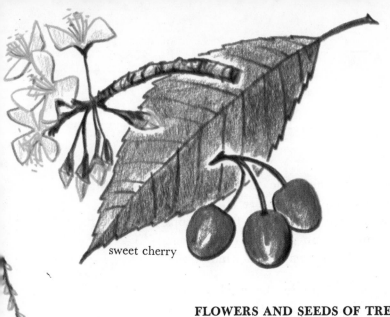

sweet cherry

FLOWERS AND SEEDS OF TREES

All trees have flowers and seeds. Many flowers are large and fragrant, others so small you have to look closely to find them. Try looking at a tree flower with a magnifying glass. Can you see the seeds inside? Some trees form seeds in the spring, others in the fall.

INJURIES TO TREES

Trees, one of our greatest natural resources, are easily injured. Thoughtless people peel or cut into bark with their knives. Fires damage or destroy whole forests. Gale winds tear off branches, and hurricanes knock trees to the ground. Insects injure trees by eating leaves or boring into trunks or roots.

A tree can heal a small injury in a few years. The growing layer under the bark spreads out over the injury, leaving only a scar. The larger injury, the longer it takes to heal.

287

Plants

It is almost impossible to walk outside without seeing one member of the plant kingdom. You see them in flower shops, in vacant lots, in gardens, on a desert, in woods, by the water, on window sills.

What flowers are in the yard of your meeting place or along the street? Flowers are not just to look at. They have a job to do. Insects live on the nectar from flowers. Bees make honey from the nectar to feed their young. If some troop members have never tasted honey, try it at a meeting.

The color and odor of plants attract insects to them. As the insects brush against the pollen in flowers, it sticks to their legs. Then they carry the pollen from one flower to another and make it possible for seeds to form.

Did you know that your kitchen is full of plant seeds? Corn, peas, beans—all these are seeds of some plant. Can you list other foods that come from plants?

You can grow plants by making cuttings. Cut off a stalk of a flower or bush. Put this cutting in water. After the stalk has grown roots in the water, plant it in soil.

PLANT OBSERVATION GAME

How many of these plants can your patrol find? Look at the plants but do not pick them. They will not last long, and other people cannot enjoy them as you did.

- ☐ A plant covering up a scar on the earth.
- ☐ A plant growing in the shade.
- ☐ A plant growing in the sun.
- ☐ A plant growing in water or a moist place.
- ☐ A plant growing in a dry place.
- ☐ A plant with flowers all one color, two, three.
- ☐ A plant that smells like perfume.
- ☐ A flower smaller than a penny.
- ☐ A flower bigger than a quarter.
- ☐ A plant from another part of the world.
- ☐ A plant with a sticky or fuzzy stem.
- ☐ A plant with shiny leaves.
- ☐ A plant with leaves bigger than the flower.
- ☐ A plant with a round flower.
- ☐ A plant with a flower shaped like a horn.
- ☐ A golden flower.
- ☐ A plant with seeds.
- ☐ A plant with buds.
- ☐ A plant with leaves shaped like trefoils.
- ☐ A plant with fruit.
- ☐ A plant that eats insects.
- ☐ A prickly plant.
- ☐ A plant that has attracted an insect to look for nectar.
- ☐ A plant that animals or birds or people like to eat.

. . . in the woods

. . . in gardens

. . . in the fields

. . . in the hou

. . . in the desert

. . . in rocks

YOU CAN FIND FLOWERS ANYWHERE YOU LOOK...

. . . in water

Rocks and Minerals

What rocks and minerals have you used today? Have you worn any? Stepped on any? Did you feel any? Did they feel soft or hard? Smooth or rough? What color were they?

You used graphite when you used a lead pencil. When you write, it is not "lead" but the mineral graphite that marks your paper. The buildings you passed may have been made with marble or granite or limestone.

If you used talcum powder, you used the mineral talc. In its natural state, it is so soft you can scratch it with your finger nail. Another soft mineral you may have used today is salt.

Did you buy anything today? Pennies are made from copper, "nickels" from nickel, dimes from silver. Gold is used for money and also in jewelry. Plaster of Paris, used to cast animal tracks, is made from alabaster.

Most minerals took millions and millions of years to make. Limestone comes from the bones and shells of animals that lived millions of years ago. Coal was formed by plants and ferns that grew millions of years ago. Fossils are the skeletons or casts of ancient animals and plants.

In your home, everywhere you go you find rocks and minerals. If you make a rock collection see pages 213-215 for ideas on arranging it. Your troop could make up a game about rocks and minerals like the Tree Game on page 284.

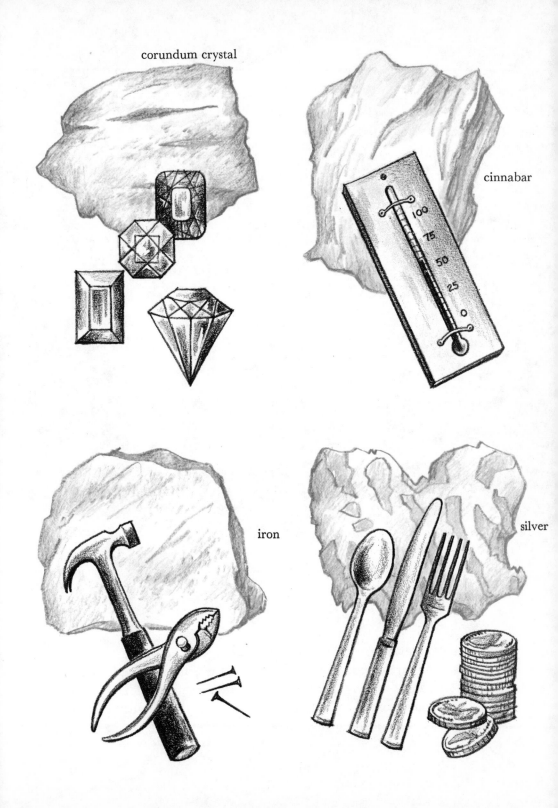

corundum crystal

cinnabar

iron

silver

Space and Stars

What is space like? It is dark and quiet and cold. There is no air far out in space. Air and the particles in air reflect light like tiny mirrors. The earth's blanket of air carries sound and absorbs heat, but there is nothing to carry sound or hold heat out in space.

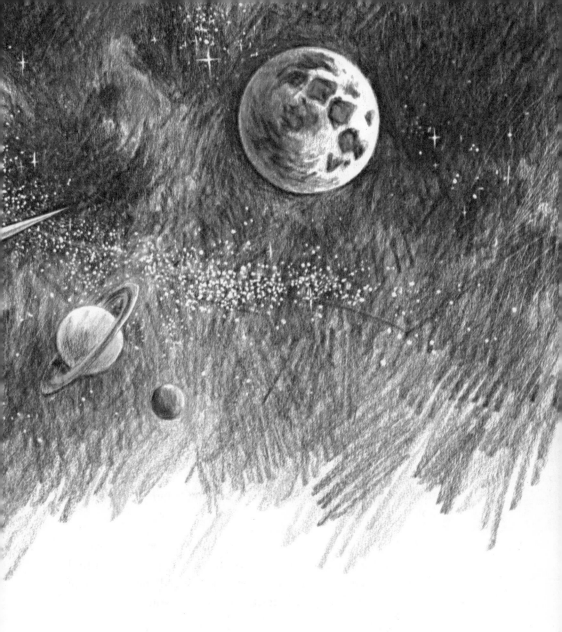

There are billions of clusters of stars in space. These clusters are called galaxies. Our sun is part of the galaxy we call the Milky Way. On a clear night, look up at the sky and see the milky white band of light from millions of stars going from northeast to southwest. Space is so big, it is hard to imagine that our sun and earth belong to the Milky Way.

A STORY BOOK IN THE SKY

Long ago men told stories in the evening after the day's work was done. They looked up at the dark skies and named groups of stars after the heroes and animals and objects in their stories. These groups of stars are called constellations, which means "stars together."

At a night troop meeting and at camp look for constellations. The Big Dipper is a good one to start with because the handle and edges of the dipper point to other constellations.

Before you go out, study a sky chart so you know what to look for. Then make a chart of the constellations by pinning paper stars in correct position on a dark blanket.

In a dark room, someone could tell one of the old star legends. The rest of the troop can form the constellations with their own stars made out of flashlights.

You can make a star theatre by punching holes with a pin in the bottom of a carton, and then shining a light through the holes.

Did you know that you could get direction from the North Star and the sun if you do not have a compass? Once you find out where north is and face north, south will be in back of you, east will be on your right and west on your left.

* At night you can see the North Star in the Little Dipper. When you face the North Star, you are facing north.

* In the morning the sun is in the east. Your shadow points west.

* In the afternoon the sun is in the west. Your shadow points east.

Weather

All around you is a layer of air. You can feel it. It is air that makes our weather. When the air is warm the thermometer goes up, and you feel warm. When the air is cold, the thermometer dips low, and you feel cold. When the air moves quickly, it is windy. Every time the air changes, our weather changes.

Air soaks up water like a giant sponge. Tiny drops of water gather on tiny bits of dust in the air and together form a cloud. When the drops get big, they fall back to earth in the form of rain, sleet, snow, or hail. In the center of every rain drop is a particle of dust. Did you know that fog is a cloud close to the ground?

Here are some clues from the wind and clouds:

If the WIND is blowing from	and the CLOUDS are	then the WEATHER is apt to be
W or NW to N	Cirrus	Good
NE or E to S	Cirrus	Rainy or snowy in a day or two if the wind is steady.
NE or E to S	Cumulus	Fair—but if these clouds build up, they may bring a storm.
NE or E to S	Cumulonimbus	Rainy soon, thunderstorm.
NE to S	Stratus	Rainy or snowy in fifteen or twenty hours, usually a steady rain.
Westerly	Stratus	Overcast sky or light drizzle.

Conservation

When you made your Girl Scout Promise, you gave your word to do your duty to your country. Your country includes all things growing and living in it.

THE CONSERVATION PLEDGE

I give my pledge as an American
to save and faithfully to defend from waste
the natural resources of my country—its soil
and minerals, its forests, waters and wildlife.

When you see in the woods a sign that says "Lou Henry Hoover Memorial Wildlife Sanctuary," you will know that Girl Scouts are carrying out plans to protect and help wildlife and plants in that area.

These conservation projects are a memorial to Lou Henry Hoover, the wife of former President Herbert Hoover. Mrs. Hoover was once president of Girl Scouts of the U.S.A. and shared her love of camping and the out-of-doors with thousands of Girl Scouts.

Throughout the United States there are many wildlife sanctuaries, nature centers, state and national parks and forests where plants and animals can grow and live in a protected place. Is there one near you?

OUTDOOR GOOD TURNS

Wherever you go, you can do outdoor good turns—by yourself or with your troop or unit.

* Do not pick wild flowers and plants. Wild flowers do not last long if they are picked.
* Give plants water when the soil is dry.
* Leave gates as you find them, either open or closed.
* Walk carefully so you do not crush plants or animal homes. When your troop comes to an untrampled field, do not all hike through the same place. Spread out so you leave the field just as it was when you came.
* Prevent erosion by not making paths straight up a hillside. On a hike walk up a hill zigzag. The tramping of many feet straight up and down a hill may start a path. The path becomes a gully when rain water runs down the path and takes the soil with it. This also makes streams muddy.
* Rope off bare spots or paths on your camp site with roots exposed, or any other spot that has no grass or plants on it. Then people will not walk there, and plants will have a chance to grow there again.
* Plant flowers or grass on bare spots, so the ground will not blow or wash away. Are there any spots where you live that Girl Scouts plant and care for? Around your meeting place? Town square? Camp site?
* Always practice fire safety rules.
* Cut sticks only in a place where there are many other bushes or trees. Cut close to the ground.
* Always leave any place—street or camp site—better than you found it. Put litter in trash cans. Make car litter bags to use in keeping the highways beautiful.

PREVENT
ACCIDENTS

Girl Scouts have often helped people because they were prepared to act in case of accident. They have even saved lives. This chapter tells you how to "be prepared" for safety.

When a person does not know a safety rule or how to use a tool, toy, bicycle or other equipment correctly, she puts herself and others in danger. Sometimes one person dares another to do something reckless. If a person does something she knows is reckless, she is not being brave. She is being foolish. When your parents and your troop or camp leader see that you know how to follow safety rules, they know they can trust you to take care of yourself and other people.

When accidents happen, people get excited and do not think clearly. And you might get excited, too, if you did not know just what to do. In your troop meetings, practice first aid and what to do in case of accident. Find out where the nearest hospital and doctor are in case you ever need to call, or direct another person. Practice until you are sure that you know what to do.

Games are a good way to prepare yourself. Choose one team to be the people in trouble and another team to be Girl Scouts ready to help. The leader calls out accidents. "Flames in the house!" "This person feels faint." "A twisted ankle." Change sides for each new situation.

Play a wide game with the accidents described in this chapter. Have at each station along the trail players who need a certain kind of help. The rest of the players must help the people they meet at each station in order to get the clue to the next station along the trail.

First Aid Kit

Your troop needs a first aid kit to be prepared to care for cuts and scratches or injuries that may happen at a meeting or on a hike or trip. Of course a doctor should always take care of serious injuries. But first aid can make the patient more comfortable until she sees the doctor.

If you or any troop member has an accident, tell your leader immediately. When you have learned how, the leader may tell you to take care of the injury and put on a bandage while she watches. Usually it will be better for your leader to care for it.

Use a tin lunch box or a candy box for the kit. A strap with a handle makes the box easy to carry and keeps it closed. Fill the kit with supplies to care for the kind of accident that may happen to your troop depending on what you do and where you live. The next page is a suggested list. Label everything in the kit so that anyone who uses it will know exactly what is in each bottle or tube.

TROOP FIRST AID KIT		
	BITES STINGS	Bicarbonate of soda (dissolve in water to use)
	BLISTERS	Soap Adhesive dressings
	BURNS	Sterile dressing
	FAINTING	Aromatic spirits of ammonia inhaling capsules
	PLANT POISONING	Soap Calamine lotion
	CUTS SKINNED KNEES OR ELBOWS SCRATCHES	Soap Adhesive compresses Sterile dressing Adhesive
	SPRAINS	Triangular bandage
	SPLINTERS	Package of needles Matches for sterilizing needle
	ANY EMERGENCY	Small pair of scissors Safety pins Change for telephone call First aid book

First Aid

* Always wash your hands before giving first aid.

* Wash wound carefully with soap and water.

* Do not touch wound with fingers, clothing, or any other object.

* Do not breathe directly or cough over the wound.

* When you open the package of a sterile dressing, hold the dressing by a corner so you do not touch the part that will go over the open wound. Cover wound with sterile dressing. Apply bandage to hold dressing in place. Send for doctor.

SHOCK

An injured person often develops "shock." His skin is pale and moist. He is weak.

Keep the person lying down and warm and quiet. Cover him with a blanket or coat. If an injured person is not already in shock, this treatment will help prevent shock. When in doubt, "Treat for shock and call the doc."

SCRATCH OR CUT

1. Wash the cut or scratch carefully and thoroughly, using soap and clean water. Use a sterile dressing as a washcloth.

2. Put a dry sterile dressing over the cut. This will protect it from infection. Put the adhesive tape on skin that is not injured, never on the cut. Do not use cotton.

BURNS

For minor burns (skin is just reddened), put the burned area in cold water, then apply a sterile dressing. *For bad burns* (skin is burned off or badly blistered), cover the burned area with a sterile dressing.

SUNBURN

The sun can burn skin, too. Sunburn can be as painful as a burn from a hot object. The first few times that you go swimming or wear summer clothing, do not stay in the sun too long. Put on a long sleeved shirt and slacks or move into the shade. Put cold cream on sunburned skin and stay out of the sun until soreness is completely gone.

BLISTERS

1. Gently wash the skin where the blister is. Do not break the blister.
2. Put on a sterile dressing and bandage.

SOMETHING IN THE EYE

Do not rub your eye when you get something in it, for the object may scratch the eye. Get help from an adult.

PLANT POISONING

1. Learn to recognize plants that are poisonous to touch. Poison ivy, poison oak, and poison sumac all grow in this country. In Florida, poison wood grows.

2. Stay away from them. Warn anyone with you to stay away.

3. If you have come in contact with one of these plants, wash yourself thoroughly with soap and water. If a rash appears and it is itchy, apply calamine lotion and see a doctor.

BRUISES

A bruise turns "black and blue" because little blood vessels under the skin have been broken. When someone has been hurt and you think there will be a bruise, put cold, wet cloths on the spot right away. This helps keep the swelling down and eases the pain.

SPLINTERS

Sterilize a needle by holding the tip in the flame of a match. Wipe the needle with sterile gauze. Use the needle to gently lift the skin over the splinter. Remove the splinter by sliding it out with the needle, or use tweezers. Cover the opening of the wound with a sterile dressing.

306

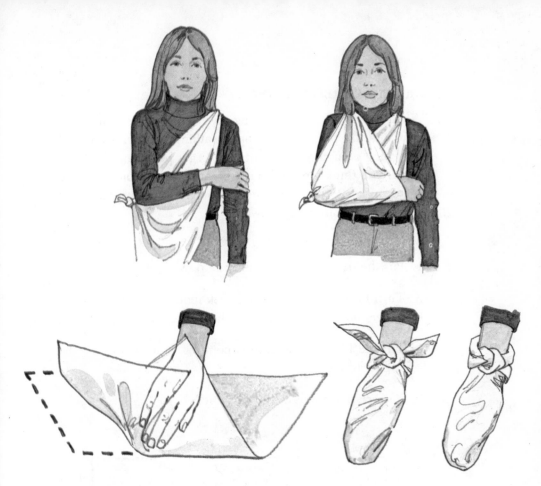

THREE WAYS TO USE A TRIANGULAR BANDAGE

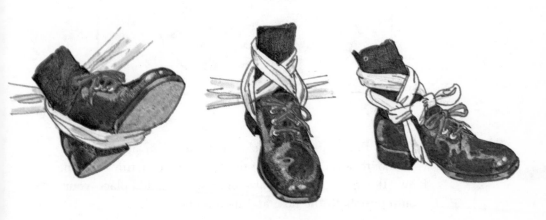

307

ARTIFICIAL RESPIRATION

When someone stops breathing give artificial respiration immediately. A person may stop breathing after choking and strangling or after an accident such as gas poisoning or drowning. If you think a person is not breathing, put your ear close to her nose. If you do not hear air coming in and out, start artificial respiration right away.

Mouth-to-mouth breathing

1. Put the person on her back lying down.

2. Turn head to the side and check mouth. Quickly remove from her mouth things such as chewing gum, food, seaweed.

3. Tilt the head so the chin is pointing upward toward the ceiling or sky.

4. Push or pull the jaw so it juts out.

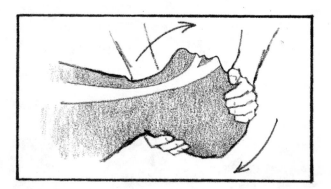

5. Pinch the victim's nose closed if she is an adult. Open your mouth wide and place it tightly over the victim's mouth. Blow. If the victim is a baby or a small child, place your mouth over both the nose and mouth and blow.

6. Turn your head and listen for air to come out. If you do not hear air come out, you did not get air down the passage to the lungs. Quickly check her head position and mouth. Blow again. If you still do not hear the air, quickly roll the victim on her side and hit her between the shoulder blades to try and clear the air passage.

7. When you hear the air leave the victim's mouth, begin to blow regularly into her mouth. Blow, then turn your head and take a big breath of air yourself. Blow into her mouth again. Blow twelve times a minute. Blow hard into a big person's mouth. Blow short puffs into a baby's mouth at about twenty times per minute.

Do not stop until the victim is breathing by herself. Do not leave the person. If she stops breathing, begin again.

At your troop meeting, practice breathing twelve times per minute, twenty times per minute. Time yourselves. It is not necessary to practice actually blowing into a person's mouth if you know step by step what to do.

Other methods of artificial respiration are described in the supplement on artificial respiration of the *American National Red Cross First Aid Textbook*. Ask your leader or some other adult to teach you how to do these.

FAINTING

When a person faints, her eyes close; she slumps or falls. She breathes, but does not hear. A person may faint from hunger, tiredness, fear, being in a crowded room, the sight of blood, or from pain.

1. Help the person to a lying down position and keep her there. She needs more blood in her brain. The heart can pump blood to the head more easily when she is lying down because blood does not have to go uphill.

2. The person usually opens her eyes quickly and soon recovers. Get help.

When someone feels as if she were going to faint, help more blood get to her brain in one of these ways:

* Help the person to lie down and tell her to breathe deeply.

* Help the person to sit down and put her head between her knees and tell her to breathe deeply.

* Help her kneel on one knee and put her head down. Tell her to breathe deeply.

FIRE

In your troop, practice what to do

If your clothes catch on fire

1. Drop to the ground. Never run! If you run, you give the fire more oxygen and the fire burns faster.
2. Cover your face with your hands.
3. Roll over slowly to shut out the oxygen. If there is a woolen coat or blanket at hand, wrap it around you to smother the flames.

If another person's clothes catch on fire

1. Get the person to the ground. Roll him over.
2. Wrap a woolen coat or blanket around the person to smother the flames.
3. Take care that your own clothing does not catch fire.

If fire breaks out in your home

1. Get yourself and other people out of the house.
2. Go to nearest telephone or alarm box and call fire department. Give your name and address. If you call from an alarm box, stay there to direct fire truck when it arrives.

If smoke comes into the room and the door is closed

1. Do not open the door. Feel it.
2. If it is hot, block the crack under the door with a rug. Go to the window and call for help. Stay by the window.
3. If the door is cool, open it a little and brace it with your foot. Do not stick your head out until you feel the air outside with your hand. If the air is not hot, walk out of the house immediately.

Fire safety outdoors is described in the "Fires" chapter. Fire safety in the kitchen is described on page 134.

SWIMMING

If you have not yet learned to swim well, stay where you can easily touch bottom and wade to shore. Know how deep the water is and whether there is anything under the surface —logs and rocks for instance—before diving.

Always swim with a buddy. Enter and leave the swimming area together. You are each other's special guard.

Always swim where there is a lifeguard and rescue equipment—a ring buoy and boats. Follow the rules where you are swimming. Do not shove or push other swimmers. Call for help only when you need help. When someone calls for help, get a lifeguard immediately.

Leave the water before you become tired or cold. After a meal wait an hour and a half before you go into the water.

ICE SKATING

Skate only on ice that has been tested. Keep candy and gum wrappers off the ice as such papers can make skaters fall. Always skate with a buddy. Stay in your own course.

Before you start to skate, collect something you could use to help a skater who fell through the ice—a pole, a plank, or a board tied to a rope.

If a skater falls through the ice, keep away from the thin ice or you may fall in, too. Slide your rescue equipment out to the skater and tell her to hang on to it and wriggle onto solid ice. Then you can pull her toward you. If *you* fall through, kick your feet and wriggle onto solid ice.

BICYCLING

1. Check your bicycle. The seat should be high enough that your leg is almost straight when the ball of your foot is on the pedal. Grips on the handle bars should be tight, so they do not slip. Tires should be checked often. Bolts and screws need to be tightened occasionally and parts should be oiled. Be sure your brakes are working well.

2. Have lights—both a white head light on the front and a reflector danger signal on the rear. Have some kind of signal —bell or horn—to warn people that you are coming.

3. Keep to the right. Always ride in single file. If your whole troop goes riding, ride in groups of five or six with at least 100 feet between groups so cars can pass.

4. Ride in a straight line in traffic.

5. Obey all traffic rules—red and green lights, one-way streets, stop signs. Slow down at crossings. Look both ways before crossing. Use proper hand signals (see page 158).

6. Give pedestrians the right of way. Do not bicycle on sidewalks unless you have to. If you do, be very careful.

7. Watch for cars pulling out and doors opening suddenly.

8. Never carry other riders on your bicycle. Carry only small packages in a basket or fastened to the bicycle.

9. Never show off or race in traffic, or "hitch" rides.

Bicycle tests show how well you can control your bicycle. Try the game Wheel Whiz on page 158. For a booklet of tests, write to the Bicycle Institute of America, Inc., 122 East 42nd Street, New York, New York 10017.

BRIDGES IN GIRL SCOUTING

You are a Junior Girl Scout, eleven years old, or in the sixth grade, and you have come to a bend in the path of Girl Scouting. What comes next? Cadette Girl Scouting! How do you get there? You cross a bridge.

Bridges advance Girl Scouts from Brownie troops to Junior troops and then to Cadette and Senior troops. When a girl crosses a Girl Scout bridge, she meets Girl Scouts who are older than she is. They show her some of the more advanced things she can do when she joins a troop of older girls.

YOUR BRIDGE TO CADETTE SCOUTING

During your last few months as a Junior Scout, you will probably be invited to visit a Cadette troop.

Maybe there will be a First Class Girl Scout in the troop you visit. To become First Class, a Cadette must meet four

314

Challenges and earn at least six Cadette badges. Challenges test a Cadette's ability to meet an emergency, to carry out a social event, to know the duties of a citizen, to live up to the Girl Scout Promise. As a Junior Scout you have learned something about all these areas of Scouting. As a Cadette you learn more and do much more on your own.

Look for Challenge pins on a Cadette Scout's badge sash. You will find these pins in the space below the membership stars, above the place for the Sign of the Arrow and the Sign of the Star. The First Class badge goes in the center of the four Challenge pins. You have left space for these on your sash. The Challenge pins and First Class badge you earn as a Cadette will go in that space.

Cadette badges have gold borders where Junior badges are green. Cadette badges have more requirements and take longer to earn than Junior badges. They will fill in the bottom of your badge sash and then go up the back of it.

Your experience as a patrol member in your troop will help you become a good member of a Cadette patrol. Sometimes many Cadette troops get together for a special event. Ask the Scouts you visit about their special Cadette events.

At a Rededication Ceremony in a Cadette troop, you will become a Cadette Girl Scout.

Before you become a Cadette Scout, do a Good Turn for your Junior troop. You can do this with the other girls who are ready to become Cadettes. It is fun to keep your Good Turn a secret until you are ready to present it to the troop. You might give your troop something that you liked to use, so new Junior Scouts can use it next year. This might be a quiz; a wide game; Name-It cards you made to add to your troop's game collection; poems you wrote to use in ceremonies; a piece of troop equipment you have painted or repaired; a favorite recipe for a campfire snack, a stew or a party punch.

THE BROWNIES' BRIDGE TO JUNIOR SCOUTING

Invite Brownie Girl Scouts who are ready to cross the bridge to Junior Scouting to attend one of your troop meetings. Brownies will be eager to find out what older Scouts, like you, do at meetings.

At your troop meeting, explain the insignia on your badge sash and show the Brownies your *Handbook*. Ask the Brownies to attend your patrol meeting so they begin to find out about the patrol system. Brownies do not have patrols in their troops, so this will be new to them. The Promise that Brownies make is simpler than your Promise, and they do not have the Law. In a ceremony or game or dramatics, tell the Brownies about your Promise and Law.

If you go to the same school or live close to a Brownie, you can be her special buddy and help her learn the Promise and Law. Show her pictures of your troop, things you have made. Introduce her to your patrol leader.

Brownies will feel important when you call them by name at school, wherever you see them. They like having a Junior Scout for a friend.

BADGE REQUIREMENTS

You will find the requirements for all the Junior Scout badges on the following pages. They are in the order listed below. Read the purposes of many badges before you decide which one you want to work on. The purpose tells you what you will be able to do when you have earned the badge. The "Badges" chapter will tell you more about earning badges.

Active Citizen	Hospitality	Personal Health
Art in the Round	Housekeeper	Pets
Backyard Fun	Indian Lore	Prints
Books	Magic Carpet	Rambler
Collector	Musician	Sewing
Community Safety	My Camera	Skater
Cook	My Community	Songster
Cyclist	My Home	Storyteller
Dabbler	My Trefoil	Toymaker
Dancer	My Troop	Troop Camper
Drawing & Painting	Needlecraft	Troop Dramatics
Folklore	Observer	Water Fun
Foot Traveler	Our Own Troop's	Weaving & Basketry
Gypsy	_____Badge	World Neighbor
Health Aid	Outdoor Cook	World Games
Home Health & Safety	Pen Pal	Writer

Active Citizen

Purpose: To find out about and put into practice the responsibilities of a citizen of the U.S.A.

When you complete a requirement, have leader initial and date it.

1. Show how to use and care for the flag of the U.S.A. Plan and carry out a flag ceremony.

_____

2. Explain how a person becomes a citizen of the U.S.A., and how a person may lose citizenship.

_____

3. Act out ways the Girl Scout Law can help you carry out the responsibilities of a citizen.

_____

4. Discover things your family has helped to pay for in your town by paying taxes. What responsibilities do you have when you use these things?

_____

5. Find out about some of the government agencies that serve you and your family. Visit one of them. OR Look up three local laws governing such things as bicycles, fire building, pets. Find out why these laws were made and how they serve everyone.

Sheriffs Office
J.R. 10/16/79

6. Think about and discuss how you and your family used these freedoms during the past weeks: Freedom of religion. Freedom of speech. Freedom of the press. Freedom of assembly.

_____

7. Plan ways that your troop could help adults get people to vote.

J.R. - 9/11/79

My signature_____

Leader's signature_____Date badge completed_____

Art in the Round

Purpose: To make sculpture from different materials.

When you complete a requirement, have leader initial and date it.

1. Choose four materials from the following list and find out what kind of equipment and other supplies are needed to work with each: Clay. Wire. Soft wood. Papier mâché. Prepared sculpture material.

_____

2. Show that you know how to care for and use materials and equipment chosen in No. 1.

_____

3. Make something out of each of your four materials: Animal or storybook characters, interesting shapes, mobiles or stabiles.

_____

4. Visit a museum, gallery, studio, or other place where sculpture in different materials is exhibited.

_____

5. Make one finished piece of sculpture designed for a certain place, purpose, or person. Use one or a combination of the materials in the above list.

_____

6. Display your art in the round at a troop meeting or at an exhibit.

_____

My signature_____

Leader's signature_____Date badge completed_____

Backyard Fun

Purpose: To learn and practice the things you need for outings in yards and parks.

Dates of outings

1. Help your family, patrol, or other group plan and carry out three outings. Help prepare two different sites. Use family, troop, or public equipment such as outdoor stoves, picnic tables, fireplaces.

1. _9/15/79_

2. _____

3. _____

_____

2. Plan one meal or snack that needs no cooking, one that lets each person cook, one that you cook for a group. Help plan, buy, pack, carry, prepare, and serve the food. Help clean up.

_9/14/79_

3. Make a piece of equipment such as a sit-upon, vagabond stove, emergency fuel, litterbag for family car, or toasting fork.

_7_

4. Show you can make a fire, use it, put it out, and leave fire site in good condition.

_____

5. Help plan, assemble, and pack equipment for a first aid kit.

_9/14/79_

6. Come to each of the outings in No. 1. dressed for the expected weather and for activities planned.

_____

7. Get acquainted with six natural things—tree, insect, animal, flower—you find on your outings. Do an outdoor good turn that will attract and protect birds or animals or will help plants or trees grow.

_____

8. Make a leaf print, track cast, sketch or photograph of something you find outdoors.

_9/15/79_

9. Include games, songs, campfires in your outings.

_9/15/79_

10. List the things you have learned to do for this badge that will be useful to you when you go on your next outing.

_____

My signature_____

Leader's signature_____Date badge completed_____

Books

Purpose: To find out about different kinds of books, how to use them, and how to care for them.

1. With the help of someone who knows books, make a reading plan to use in the library in your school or community.

2. Read three different kinds of books: Travel, mystery, biography, adventure, or history.

3. For your troop make an exhibit of books about an activity you are working on such as nature or arts. OR Prepare for the troop a list of books that would be useful in troop activities.

4. Visit your school or public library to find out how to: Find a book through the card catalog. Use reference books to find answers to questions. Find magazine articles about special subjects. Use dictionary and encyclopedia. Find the publisher and price of a certain book.

5. Show your troop illustrations from several books you like. Explain why you like the illustrations.

6. Start a book collection of your own. Know how to care for them and how to mend them when necessary.

7. Tell how books were made in the days before printing. OR Make a bookplate for your book collection. OR Bind a book.

My signature_____

Leader's signature_____Date badge completed_____

Collector

Purpose: To start, or add to, a collection of things you like and to arrange that collection so it will be interesting to others.

When you complete a requirement, have leader initial and date it.

1. Start a collection or add to one you have already started.

2. Figure out a way to arrange your collection at home. Use scrapbooks, shelves, boxes, or whatever seems best for the collection.

3. Group or label the objects in your collection so they will be interesting to other people.

4. Choose three objects and write a display label for each telling such things as: Where you found it. Age of object. How it was made. Story about it.

5. Find out more about your collection in one of the following ways: Visit another collector to see his or her exhibit. Read books and magazines. Talk to someone who knows about what you are collecting.

6. Show your troop your newest addition and one of your favorite pieces in your collection.

7. Display your collection at a troop meeting or hobby show, or invite some troop members to see your collection at home.

My signature_____

Leader's signature_____Date badge completed_____

322

Community Safety

Purpose: To discover how your community protects its citizens and to do your part to make it safe.

When you complete a requirement, have leader initial and date it.

1. Know four services in your community or state that protect you and your family. Visit a branch of one of these and learn what they do and how to call for them in an emergency.

JR. 10/16/79

2. List safety practices to follow on a hike and follow them on a neighborhood hike. OR Ask the police department or other community group to help you plan bicycle tests for children in your neighborhood.

JR – 9/15/79

3. Demonstrate or make an exhibit of safety rules for your playground, yard, troop meeting place, community center, or swimming pool. Observe these rules yourself and be a good example for younger children.

4. Describe an accident that happened on public property, and discuss with others how this accident might have been prevented.

JR 9/15/79

5. Discuss: The right things to do if you are approached by a stranger. Safety steps to take with discarded refrigerators and large plastic bags. How to call the nearest poison control center in an emergency.

JR 9/15/79

6. Organize and carry out with others a home or neighborhood safety project, using safety facts you have learned.

JR

My signature_____

Leader's signature_____Date badge completed_____

323

Cook

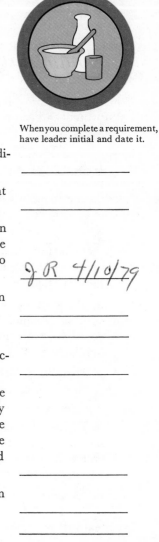

Purpose: To learn how to cook so you can fix meals for your family.

1. Show how to measure dry, liquid, and solid ingredients. Know measuring equivalents.

_____

2. Demonstrate how to: Control top burners. Preheat oven. Clean your stove safely. Use five cooking tools.

_____

3. With your patrol list the name and meaning of ten cooking and food terms that are new to you. Name the basic four food groups and why each is important to you, and plan four menus using them.

_J_ _R_ _4/10/79_

4. Show that you know how to "clean up as you go" in cooking and how to store food.

_____

5. Learn the history of your favorite food or spice.

_____

6. Bake a cake from a prepared mix by following directions on the package. Frost it.

_____

7. Learn how to prepare the following foods and use them in planning meals: One starchy and one leafy vegetable as a side dish. One fresh vegetable salad. One cooked fruit dessert. One fresh fruit for breakfast. White sauce or a milk dessert. Two main dishes of ground beef, fish, cheese, or eggs.

_____

8. Learn how to use three kinds of cereal products in meals, and prepare a dish using one of them.

_____

9. Describe three well balanced lunches you enjoy.

_____

10. Plan and prepare a simple, well balanced dinner for your family or patrol.

_____

My signature_____

Leader's signature_____Date badge completed_____

Cyclist

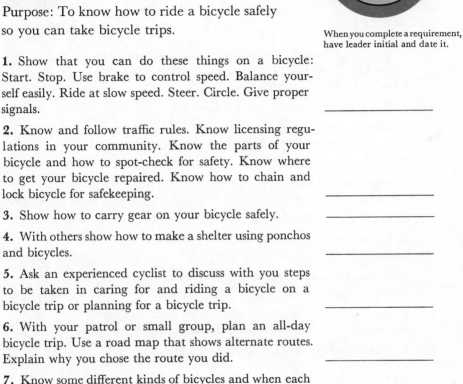

Purpose: To know how to ride a bicycle safely so you can take bicycle trips.

When you complete a requirement, have leader initial and date it.

1. Show that you can do these things on a bicycle: Start. Stop. Use brake to control speed. Balance yourself easily. Ride at slow speed. Steer. Circle. Give proper signals.

2. Know and follow traffic rules. Know licensing regulations in your community. Know the parts of your bicycle and how to spot-check for safety. Know where to get your bicycle repaired. Know how to chain and lock bicycle for safekeeping.

3. Show how to carry gear on your bicycle safely.

4. With others show how to make a shelter using ponchos and bicycles.

5. Ask an experienced cyclist to discuss with you steps to be taken in caring for and riding a bicycle on a bicycle trip or planning for a bicycle trip.

6. With your patrol or small group, plan an all-day bicycle trip. Use a road map that shows alternate routes. Explain why you chose the route you did.

7. Know some different kinds of bicycles and when each kind is most useful.

8. With your troop, patrol, or other group, plan and carry out a troop, school, or community safety project.

My signature_____

Leader's signature_____Date badge completed_____

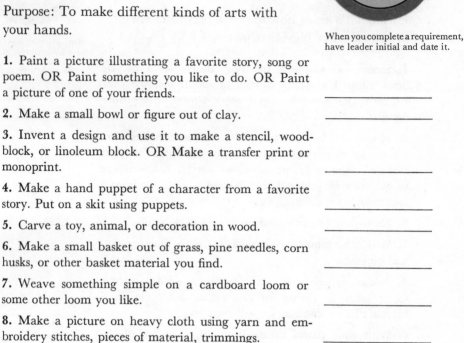

Dabbler

Purpose: To make different kinds of arts with your hands.

1. Paint a picture illustrating a favorite story, song or poem. OR Paint something you like to do. OR Paint a picture of one of your friends.

_____

2. Make a small bowl or figure out of clay.

_____

3. Invent a design and use it to make a stencil, wood-block, or linoleum block. OR Make a transfer print or monoprint.

_____

4. Make a hand puppet of a character from a favorite story. Put on a skit using puppets.

_____

5. Carve a toy, animal, or decoration in wood.

_____

6. Make a small basket out of grass, pine needles, corn husks, or other basket material you find.

_____

7. Weave something simple on a cardboard loom or some other loom you like.

_____

8. Make a picture on heavy cloth using yarn and embroidery stitches, pieces of material, trimmings.

_____

9. Make a collage, mobile, or paper sculpture.

_____

My signature_____

Leader's signature_____Date badge completed_____

Dancer

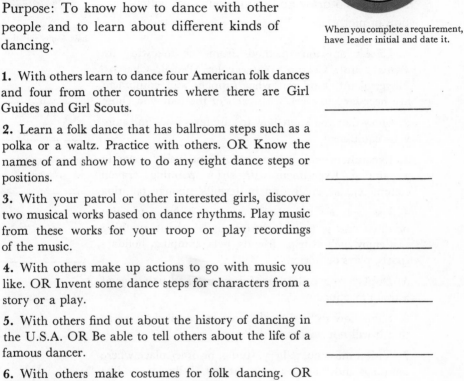

Purpose: To know how to dance with other people and to learn about different kinds of dancing.

When you complete a requirement, have leader initial and date it.

1. With others learn to dance four American folk dances and four from other countries where there are Girl Guides and Girl Scouts.

_____

2. Learn a folk dance that has ballroom steps such as a polka or a waltz. Practice with others. OR Know the names of and show how to do any eight dance steps or positions.

_____

3. With your patrol or other interested girls, discover two musical works based on dance rhythms. Play music from these works for your troop or play recordings of the music.

_____

4. With others make up actions to go with music you like. OR Invent some dance steps for characters from a story or a play.

_____

5. With others find out about the history of dancing in the U.S.A. OR Be able to tell others about the life of a famous dancer.

_____

6. With others make costumes for folk dancing. OR Find and exhibit pictures of musical instruments used to accompany dancing in different parts of the world.

_____

7. With others learn three singing games and teach them to a group of Brownie Scouts.

_____

My signature_____

Leader's signature_____Date badge completed_____

327

Drawing and Painting

Purpose: To draw and paint your own collection of pictures.

When you complete a requirement, have leader initial and date it.

1. Choose any four methods from the following list: Poster paint. Crayon. Water color. Pencil. Charcoal. Finger paint. Find out what supplies and equipment are necessary to work with each of the four you chose.

9·N· 80'

2. Show that you know how to care for, clean, and store your equipment.

9·N·80'

3. Experiment with mixing colors and using them in a painting. Experiment with string painting, crayon etching, chalks, chalk and buttermilk, sponge painting.

9·N·80'

4. Use each of the methods you chose in No. 1 to paint or draw one picture. Pictures can be about anything you enjoy such as trips, friends, pets, camping, holidays, sports, plays or stories.

5. Display your collection of drawings and paintings at a troop meeting.

6. Show how to "fix" a charcoal or pencil drawing so that it will not smear.

7. Visit a museum, gallery, studio, or other place where paintings and drawings are exhibited. Tell why you like certain pictures best.

9·N· 80'

8. Select one of your pictures to mount for your room or to give as a gift.

9·N·80'

My signature_____

Leader's signature_____Date badge completed_____

Folklore

Purpose: To learn about American folk music, folk tales, and hand arts and how they tell some of our country's history.

When you complete a requirement, have leader initial and date it.

1. Find out about the history of your community—how things happened, its legends and stories, early arts, songs or dances of early settlers. Tell or write a story about this history.

2. With your troop or patrol, work out a play or puppet show based on one of the legends. Include simple costumes, scenery, music, and dances.

3. Act out one of the folk songs. OR Learn one of the folk dances and teach it to others.

4. Find out all you can about arts practiced in your part of the country. Make up a notebook or file about works of early craftsmen and toys made by the people in early settlements. Using ideas from these early arts, create your own design using paint, metal, clay, wood, weaving, or embroidery.

5. Find out what are the chief characteristics of folk art in one of the following: New England, Pennsylvania, the Northwest, the South, the Midwest, the Southwest. Collect pictures or make sketches that show this.

6. With your troop or patrol choose a story, legend, song, or poem that tells about the early days of our country. Plan a book together. Each one letter and illustrate some of the pages. Share this book with other troops or present it to shut-ins.

My signature_____

Leader's signature_____Date badge completed_____

Foot Traveler

Purpose: To become a good hiker, able to take care of yourself and the trails you follow.

When you complete a requirement, have leader initial and date it.

1. Have the Gypsy badge.

_____

2. With your patrol, troop, camp unit, or family, plan and go on four walking trips, three at least two miles long and one at least five miles long. Three trips should be on trails or in open country. Plan routes, get necessary permissions, come dressed for expected weather and kind of hike.

Dates of hikes
1. _9/15/79_
2. _____
3. _____
4. _____

_____

3. Get together your own hike kit with drinking cup, eating utensils, compass, jackknife, rope, sit-upon.

_J R 9/15/79_

4. Show you know how to apply the Conservation Pledge along the trails you follow.

_J R 9/15/79_

5. Plan and pack a well balanced, easy-to-carry lunch for each hike. On one hike prepare a hot drink using Buddy burner or other emergency fuel. On another, cook two things. Leave site clean.   /

_____

6. Whip and hank your own rope. Show that your knife is in good condition. Use at least two kinds of knots on your hikes.

_____

7. Use a compass to follow or lay a trail on one hike. On another hike use a street or road map. Make a sketch map of a third hike, or part of it.

_____

8. Know how to bandage an injured ankle. Know what to do in a hike emergency.

_J R 9/15/79_

9. Know four songs or read four poems about the out-of-doors. OR Know four games to play outdoors. OR Discover four things in nature that are new to you.

_J R 9/15/79_

My signature_____

Leader's signature_____Date badge completed_____

330

Gypsy

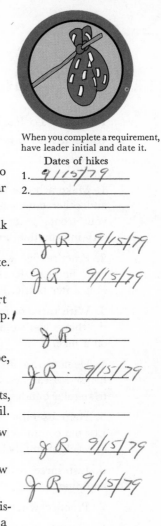

Purpose: To be able to plan and go on an all-day hike.

Dates of hikes

1. Help your patrol, troop, or camp unit plan and go on two all-day hikes. Plan where to go, what to wear and take. Get necessary permissions.

1. 9/15/79
2._____
_____

2. Know how to walk and rest correctly, how to walk in a group on street, highway, or country road.

J R 9/15/79

3. Use good outdoor manners: On the way. At hike site. On trails. Do an outdoor good turn on each hike.

J R 9/15/79

4. Plan and carry your lunch for one hike and cook part of it yourself. On the other hike cook something for a group.

_____

5. Help make and use: Fireplace. Woodpile. Fire.

J R

6. Dress for expected weather and activities. Have rope, eating utensils, and bandana.

J R . 9/15/79

7. Learn one new campcraft skill: How to tie knots, handle a knife, use a compass, or lay and follow a trail.

_____

8. Be able to teach a game to play on the way. Know a hiking song.

J R 9/15/79

9. Help keep troop first aid kit ready to use. Know what to do if you cut or burn yourself.

J R 9/15/79

10. Watch a sunset, look wide around a hilltop, or discover something interesting in nature. Find a poem or a story about the out-of-doors or about the way it makes you feel to share with your patrol.

_____

11. After each hike, talk over the hike and what you need to learn or practice before your next outing.

_____

My signature_____

Leader's signature_____Date badge completed_____

331

Health Aid

Purpose: To learn how to help take care of yourself and others when there is sickness or an accident.

1. Make a home telephone card for doctor, police, fire, and other emergency calls. Keep it by the phone. In your troop, practice making proper calls, giving necessary information, and following directions.

2. Practice five ways to help when someone is sick in your home. OR Demonstrate proper use and care of: Hot water bottle. Heating pad. Ice bag.

3. With three or four others, pantomine for your troop the things you would do to be sure of comfort and safety on a hike.

4. Demonstrate first aid for: Fainting. Small cuts. Blisters. Bruises. Scratches. Splinters. Know three ways to use a triangular bandage.

5. Help assemble a first aid kit for home or troop. OR List ten common household items that must be kept out of reach of small children and tell why.

6. List three or four rules for safe use of troop play equipment.

7. Practice what to do if someone's clothes catch fire.

8. Show how you gradually take more responsibility for your health as you grow older. Show this in a play or poster you and others plan and carry out.

My signature_____

Leader's signature_____Date badge completed_____

Home Health and Safety

Purpose: To learn and practice safety measures that will protect you and your family.

When you complete a requirement, have leader initial and date it.

1. With an adult in your family, label clearly and arrange neatly the contents of your medicine chest. OR Know and follow proper procedures for use and storage of flammable or poisonous liquids and powders, matches, and medicines found in your home. _____

2. Learn and practice the safe use of three things commonly used for each of the following: Cooking. House cleaning. Repairing. Playing. OR Select three different kinds of rooms and discuss with others what should be done in each to help keep the family safe and healthy. _____

3. List five common causes of fire in the home and steps for fire prevention. With your family, plan what you will do if there is a fire in your home. _____

4. Plan a diorama, peepshow, poster, or skit on home health and safety. OR Make and carry out a health and safety plan for your troop meeting place. _____

5. Using what you have learned, survey your home, yard, or farm and list any unsafe conditions. With the help of your family, correct as many as you can. _____

My signature_____

Leader's signature_____Date badge completed_____

Hospitality

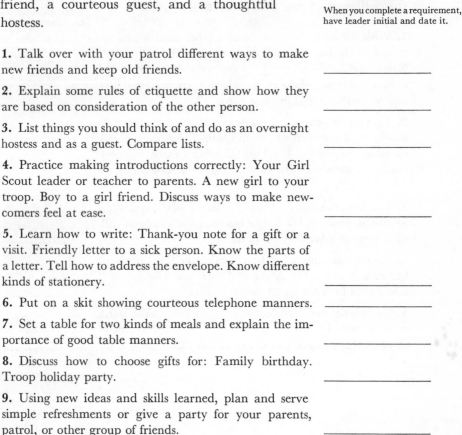

Purpose: To learn how to be an even better friend, a courteous guest, and a thoughtful hostess.

When you complete a requirement, have leader initial and date it.

1. Talk over with your patrol different ways to make new friends and keep old friends.

_____

2. Explain some rules of etiquette and show how they are based on consideration of the other person.

_____

3. List things you should think of and do as an overnight hostess and as a guest. Compare lists.

_____

4. Practice making introductions correctly: Your Girl Scout leader or teacher to parents. A new girl to your troop. Boy to a girl friend. Discuss ways to make newcomers feel at ease.

_____

5. Learn how to write: Thank-you note for a gift or a visit. Friendly letter to a sick person. Know the parts of a letter. Tell how to address the envelope. Know different kinds of stationery.

_____

6. Put on a skit showing courteous telephone manners.

_____

7. Set a table for two kinds of meals and explain the importance of good table manners.

_____

8. Discuss how to choose gifts for: Family birthday. Troop holiday party.

_____

9. Using new ideas and skills learned, plan and serve simple refreshments or give a party for your parents, patrol, or other group of friends.

_____

My signature_____

Leader's signature_____Date badge completed_____

334

Housekeeper

Purpose: To learn and use the things that must be done to keep a home pleasant, clean, and safe.

1. With your mother or leader list cleaning activities that should be done by a good housekeeper. Choose two that you will help to do each week.

2. Check the plan in your home for safe storage of cleaning equipment and supplies. Consider space, when and where they will be used, convenience, and the safety of young children.

3. Learn how to sort clothes and how they should be laundered. Describe care of Girl Scout uniform.

4. Keep a record of the money you spend for two weeks. Talk with your parents about your expenses and some possible ways to earn money.

5. Do the following: Help your mother clean the refrigerator. Show how to use a broom, dust mop, vacuum cleaner. Demonstrate a good method of dish-washing. Clean the kitchen or bathroom floor, sink and fixtures. Demonstrate bed-making. Wash a window. Clean a room thoroughly. Tell why it is important to always turn off lights, faucets, and other fixtures when you finish with them.

6. Organize your closet, drawers, and room neatly.

7. Visit grocery stores to compare labels on different food packages. Look for information on quantity, quality, and price.

8. Using the things you have learned, adopt one new housekeeping activity to do regularly.

My signature_____

Leader's signature_____Date badge completed_____

Indian Lore

Purpose: To learn about the way Indians lived in this country.

When you complete a requirement, have leader initial and date it.

1. Know the history of the Indians who once lived nearest your home. Describe their homes, costumes, and food and tell where their descendents live today. _____

2. Describe briefly the different kinds of Indians that lived in North America. Tell how their way of life was affected by the part of the country in which they lived. _____

3. Tell which states have names of Indian origin. Give the meaning of three names. _____

4. Read at least three Indian legends. Choose one and tell it to a group of Brownies or other friends. _____

5. Make a useful article such as a sheath for a knife or ax and decorate it with authentic Indian designs. OR Make a model of a tepee or other type of Indian dwelling. _____

6. Learn to play an Indian game and teach it to your patrol or troop. OR Show some Indian dance steps OR perform an Indian dance in camp or at a troop meeting. _____

7. Teach an Indian song to your patrol. Explain its meaning and how the song was used by the Indians. OR Make a simple Indian musical instrument and use it in camp or at a troop meeting. _____

My signature_____

Leader's signature_____Date badge completed_____

Magic Carpet

Purpose: To discover what you can do with stories and books to give pleasure to others.

When you complete a requirement, have leader initial and date it.

1. At a troop meeting tell about a short trip you took and what you enjoyed most about it. OR Describe something that happened to you when you went to camp or visited a relative or a friend.

2. Get your own library card or know how to apply for one. Discuss the responsibilities of having a card.

3. Pick out and read two books. Choose from folk stories, poetry, or books about animals, nature, a different country, or an American heroine.

4. Bring the book you liked best to troop meeting. Tell why you enjoyed it and read something from it. When other troop members tell about books they liked, make a list of those you would like to read.

5. Read a favorite short story or poem aloud or prepare a story and tell it as part of a troop meeting or ceremony.

6. Collect at least twelve poems that could be used in troop meetings. OR Select a story and have your patrol dramatize it.

7. Make a jacket for one of your favorite books. OR Start a library shelf or box in your troop meeting place.

8. With others plan a book illustration party at which each troop member sketches a scene from her favorite book. OR Help with a book collection drive in a community or school book project.

My signature_____

Leader's signature_____Date badge completed_____

337

Musician

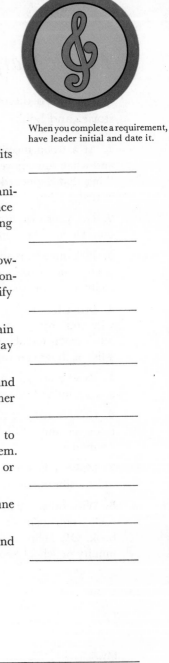

Purpose: To use your musical knowledge for troop, camp, and community events.

1. Play or sing at sight a simple piece of music. Beat its rhythm and explain all signs and terms.

_____

2. Learn to play alone or with others two accompaniments to which your troop or fellow campers can dance or sing. OR Teach an American folk song and singing game.

_____

3. Explain to your patrol what is meant by the following musical terms: Sonata. Quartet. Symphony. Concerto. Listen to examples of each until you can identify them and their composers.

_____

4. Make a simple percussion instrument. OR Explain to others how the instrument you are learning to play is made, how it works, and its range.

_____

5. As a soloist or with others, sing or play background or incidental music for a campfire, Scouts' Own, or other special event.

_____

6. Read the story of an operetta or an opera. Listen to some excerpts from it until you are familiar with them. OR With others, present a scene from an operetta or opera with friends or puppets and recordings.

_____

7. Write a simple, original tune. OR Listen to a tune and make up dance steps to it.

_____

8. Discuss good concert manners and with others attend a musical event.

_____

My signature_____

Leader's signature_____Date badge completed_____

My Camera

Purpose: To learn how to use a camera and to take pictures of many things in different lights.

1. Load your camera with film. After you have finished using the film, unload it. Explain the parts of your camera as you use it or adjust it to take a picture.

2. Make a list of the subjects you plan to photograph. Tell how far away you will stand from each.

3. Show a photograph that tells a story. Explain why it tells a story.

4. Describe how foreground and background objects can help or spoil a picture.

5. Take a time exposure or flash picture.

6. Take a series of pictures of the same subject that shows variation in light and shadow: Light behind object. Light behind camera. Light from the side. Through a doorway or branches. Close up. Far away.

7. Take pictures to use as a record of a trip or an event. OR Take pictures to tell a story and choose a title for the story.

8. Mount one or two of your best pictures. OR Start a photograph album. Write captions for the pictures.

My signature_____

Leader's signature_____ Date badge completed_____

My Community

Purpose: To find out about your community—
its history and the ways it helps the people
who live there now.

1. Find out how your community got started. Visit at
least one historic place. 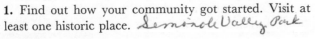 *JR – 5/79*

2. Learn when your state was admitted to the Union.
Make pictures of your state flag, flower, and bird, and
explain why each was chosen. Give your state motto and
tell what it means. _____

3. Visit a newspaper or a radio or television station to
learn how they keep your community informed of local,
national, and international news. Tell why this is important. Share at least two current events with your troop. _____

4. Locate on a map and then visit one of the public
recreation areas near where you live. Explain who
operates this area and why we have such areas. *Nature Center* *JR 5/79*

5. Plan and take part in a skit that shows how citizens
use hospitals, libraries, schools, and social agencies in
your community. Show in the skit what the community
would be like without these agencies. _____

6. Show how you would help a visitor learn about and
see some of the interesting places near you. _____

7. Take part in a service project that will help your
community. _____

My signature_____

Leader's signature_____Date badge completed_____

My Home

Purpose: To find ways to make your home a more pleasant place to live.

When you complete a requirement, have leader initial and date it.

1. List things that each family member does to help the others every day and that make your home a pleasant place to be. Discuss things you do now or you might do. Tell which Scouting activities help you to be a better member of your family.

2. Talk or write to older people and learn what they liked to do and how they lived at your age.

3. With a grownup present, play with a small child for several hours. Read a story with him. See what toys he likes and what care he needs.

4. Make something useful for your home such as hot pads, place mats, a pin cushion, a pillow top.

5. Find out how a girl of your age in another country lives and how she helps at home. OR Interest your family in trying a food of another country. Help serve it.

6. Plant and care for bulbs, flower seeds, or a house plant for a month. OR Care for a pet.

7. Plan ways to make your room more attractive: Helping to rearrange furniture, making a schedule to keep it clean, putting up or changing a picture, storing clothes.

8. Discuss with your mother some new service you could give in your home and do it.

My signature_____

Leader's signature_____ Date badge completed_____

My Trefoil

Purpose: To discover and practice more ways
to carry out the Girl Scout Promise.

When you complete a requirement,
have leader initial and date it.

1. Start a scrapbook of poems, quotations, and pictures
that illustrate: On my honor. I will try. To serve God.
(To serve) my country and mankind.

2. Learn from Girl Scout books a grace to sing and a
song for patriotic occasions.

_J R. 9/4/79_

3. Find out about customs of different religious faiths
that affect holidays, food, and activities, so that you can
respect the beliefs of other Scouts when planning activities with them.

4. Explain how the second part of the Promise—To
serve "my country and mankind"—is connected with
the Girl Scout motto, "Be Prepared," and the slogan,
"Do a good turn daily."

5. Watch to see the many things people do to help each
other. Make up charades, shadowgraphs, or a skit to
show some of the things that you observed which you
are going to do.

6. Make a list of ways you will try to live up to the Law.
Write the Law. Then think about everything you did in
one day and list beside each part of the Law those things
in which that part of the Law helped you decide how to
act. OR Cut from newspapers and magazines pictures
or stories that illustrate each part of the Law, and explain
why you chose the pictures and stories.

7. Do one or more service projects that would carry out
the Promise. 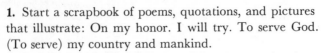 _Caroled Shut ins & Elderly JR 12/79_

My signature_____

Leader's signature_____Date badge completed_____

342

My Troop

Purpose: To become a better member of your troop so that you can do more for it.

1. Show that you know how Girl Scouting started in the U.S.A.

2. With your patrol make a chart showing how your troop is a part of its Girl Scout neighborhood, council, region, and national organization. Know the name of your council and region. Know the states in your region.

3. Explain what the two circles of the patrol leader cord stand for. Explain how you can do your part at patrol meetings and troop meetings. *J R 9/17/79*

4. Plan and carry out an opening ceremony and a closing ceremony for your troop.

5. Collect and record dues for your patrol or shop for some troop supplies. Help figure out a budget for a troop event.

6. List people who have helped your troop in the past year. Plan ways to thank them.

7. Do something to improve your troop meeting place or camp site.

8. Show how to wear your Girl Scout uniform and insignia. Explain why you should wear them neatly and correctly.

9. Invite a Cadette to tell you what her troop does. OR Help a Brownie cross the bridge to Junior Scouting. OR Take part in a Girl Scout Week activity.

My signature_____

Leader's signature_____Date badge completed_____

Needlecraft

Purpose: To learn many different stitches and use them to make or decorate articles you have designed.

When you complete a requirement, have leader initial and date it.

1. Learn four of the following: Cross stitch. Blanket stitch. Chain stitch. French knot. Satin stitch. Outline stitch. Practice using the stitches by working a picture or sampler.

g R   1/26/79

2. Decorate a household article or piece of clothing using two or more of the following: Hemstitching. Smocking stitch. Needle weaving. Darning stitch. Huck-a-back darning. Crewelwork. Knitting. Crocheting. Needlepoint.

3. Work out on graph paper a simple design for needlepoint or cross stitch.

g R   1/26/79

4. Make a small, simple design using appliqué, quilting, or hooking. OR Create a picture or design for a wall hanging or pillow cover using stitches learned in No. 1.

5. Display at a troop meeting the things you made.

My signature_____

Leader's signature_____Date badge completed_____

Observer

Purpose: To know how and why nature changes with the seasons.

When you complete a requirement, have leader initial and date it.

1. With others, take an adventure hike in a park or your neighborhood. Look for: Plants, trees, animals, reptiles, amphibians, insects. Look for them in another season. Note the changes.   *gost*

2. Find: A rock formation, three weather signs, and two cloud formations.   *gR 11/29*

3. Find out about water conservation or soil erosion. OR Make a conservation exhibit.   *gR 9/15/79*

4. Locate four constellations such as the Big and Little Dippers, Orion, Cassiopeia. Try to find them at another season of the year.

5. Plant a flower garden for birds at two different seasons of the year. OR Identify or press fall or spring leaves. OR Choose a small area, watch to see what lives there, and check it at another season for any change. Tell others what you find.   *gR 7/79*

6. Observe four of the following: Bird building its nest. Mud wasp building its nursery. Bee getting pollen or nectar from a flower. Ant carrying a load twice its size. Spider wrapping its prey with its web. Tell others what you have seen.

My signature_____

Leader's signature_____Date badge completed_____

345

Our Own Troop's Badge

When you and other members of your troop have an interest which is not included in any of the badges in this *Handbook*, you can develop a special Our Own Troop's _____ Badge on that subject. An individual girl cannot do this badge by herself. A group must make up the requirements, the name, and the symbol together. No other girls in your troop or in any other troop can use your badge. Even if they choose the same subject, they must create their own requirements and symbol.

To earn this badge:

Make sure that your chosen subject is not covered in any of the Junior badges, and that it does not conflict with the Girl Scout Promise and Law.

Ask your council for approval of your badge subject. The council approves only the subject of the badge, not its requirements.

With your leader, review the meaning and characteristics of Junior badges. Then write your own requirements on the next page, agree on a name for the badge and a design for the badge symbol. The name of your subject goes in the blank space in the title Our Own Troop's _____ Badge. Each girl puts the badge symbol the troop has designed on her own blank badge with the green border.

Do the requirements in a way that satisfies yourselves, your leader, and your consultant (if you have one for this badge).

When you have completed your badge, send a copy of the requirements and a sample cloth badge symbol to your council and to the National Program Committee at national headquarters for their information and possible display.

346

Our Own Troop's _____ *Badge*

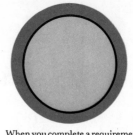

Purpose:

When you complete a requirement, have leader initial and date it.

1. _____
_____
_____
_____
_____
_____
_____
_____
_____
_____
_____
_____
_____
_____
_____
_____
_____
_____
_____
_____
_____
_____
_____
_____
_____
_____
_____
_____

My signature_____

Leader's signature_____Date badge completed_____

Outdoor Cook

Purpose: To learn how to build different fires and cook food on the fires.

1. With four to eight other girls help plan, prepare, and serve four different meals, including four different types of cooking. Help do the following in each meal: Plan balanced menus. Make shopping list. Shop. Take care of food at site. Establish eating place. Prepare and serve food. Clean up.

Dates of meals
1. _9/15/79_
2. _____
3. _____
4. _____

_____

2. Help set up and use four different types of fireplace and fire. Build and use one fire without adult help. Know correct tinder, kindling, and fuel for your locality. Show how to put fire out. Charcoal,

_____

3. Make a cooking fire in windy or wet weather.

_____

4. Use correct knots for hanging caches and dunking bags. OR Make shavings and point sticks. OR Know how to remove and replace sod. OR Make two pieces of outdoor cooking equipment.

_____

5. Have your own cooking kit. Help plan and assemble a patrol cooking kit.

_____

6. Tell about two games that could be played while meal is cooking. OR Help make a troop or unit outdoor recipe file. OR Select two eatable wild foods.

_J R. 9/15/79_

7. List five ways you have practiced good fire and cooking safety. OR Know first aid treatment for burns and cuts and tell ways these can be avoided. OR Help make a waste water drain, a garbage disposal, or a dishwashing setup.

_J R 9/15/79_

My signature_____

Leader's signature_____Date badge completed_____

Pen Pal

Purpose: To correspond with a pen pal and learn to write different kinds of letters.

When you complete a requirement, have leader initial and date it.

1. Practice writing the following to a real or imaginary friend: Thank-you note for gift or visit. Letter with news of friends or community. Account of a troop or school project. Something humorous to amuse a sick friend. Invitation to attend a party or to make a visit. Letter to a younger or an older person.

_____

2. Share these practice letters with other troop members working on the badge and exchange ideas for making each other's letters more interesting. Ask your parents, teacher, or other adult friend to help you improve the form, punctuation, writing, and neatness of your letters.

_____

3. Correspond with a pen pal—a new friend or one you do not see often. In your letters try to: Find out about her hobbies and tell her about yours. Give her news about your Girl Scout troop. Illustrate at least one letter with sketches, photographs, or pasted pictures and tell her about your family and home. Tell her about one place in your community that you like to visit.

_____

4. Practice wrapping packages securely and neatly. Show that you can address them correctly.

_____

5. After you have exchanged four or more letters with your pen pal and feel you know each other well, discuss with your leader, patrol, or troop what has made the correspondence interesting.

_____

My signature_____

Leader's signature_____Date badge completed_____

349

Personal Health

Purpose: To learn how and why to guard your own health.

When you complete a requirement, have leader initial and date it.

1. Have a health examination. Make a record of the doctor's advice and follow it.

_____

2. Make a chart showing foods necessary for a well balanced diet. Find out how these foods help to build sound teeth and strong bodies.

_____

3. Explain proper care of teeth, hair, skin, hands, and feet.

_____

4. Act out good posture in sitting, walking, standing, and lifting.

_____

5. Know five diseases from which you can be protected by inoculations. Keep a record of the inoculations you have had.

_____

6. Discuss with your troop why active games and sports are important to your health.

_____

7. Help plan and carry out a program that shows the rules of good health. Use posters, games, skits, songs, exhibits, or plays.

_____

8. Make a chart of the health steps you have learned. Check yourself on the chart for two weeks to see if you can improve your health habits.

_____

My signature_____

Leader's signature_____Date badge completed_____

350

Pets

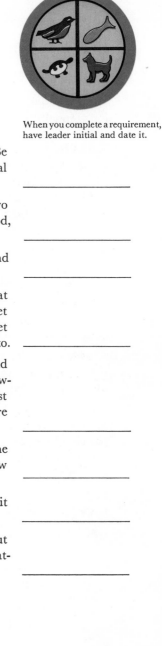

Purpose: To find out more about your pet and how you can look after it.

1. Read at least two books about your kind of pet. Be able to tell about the history of that kind of animal and others of the same family.

_____

2. Take responsibility for your pet for at least two months, providing it with the right kind of shelter, food, and exercise.

_____

3. Discuss the kinds of illness common to your pet and how you protect it against disease.

_____

4. Know what to do when you see your pet is ill: What precautions to take until help is available. How to get in touch with a veterinarian. How to give your pet medicine if your veterinarian and parents want you to.

_____

5. Tell how a female pet should be cared for before and after she has her young. Know: Kind of food the newborns need if natural food is not available. Kind of nest or bed needed. How to housebreak young if they are to be allowed in house.

_____

6. Show the proper way to carry your pet from one place to another safely. If your pet can be trained, know how to give it training directions.

_____

7. Know about a society to protect animals. OR Visit an animal shelter.

_____

8. Make a record of anything you have or know about your pet: Photographs, sketches, "shots," special treatments.

_____

My signature_____

Leader's signature_____ Date badge completed_____

351

Prints

Purpose: To make different kinds of prints for yourself and others.

1. Collect things with which to make an impression or gadget print such as: Dowel ends, screws, bottle caps, sticks, sponge, eraser. Use stamp pad. Experiment with one item at a time to create a border design, an all-over pattern, or a design in two colors.

JR 10/79

2. Make a transfer print with leaves, ferns, or bark. OR Make a rubbing of something "raised" such as: A carving; a design on an iron gate; the texture of a leaf, bark, brick, or stone.

JR 10/79

3. Make a stencil using your own design. Show safe way to use a stencil cutting tool. Paint your stenciled design on paper or fabric.

JR 10/79

4. Make a relief print. Either cut your design in a potato or other vegetable, or glue a felt, rubber, or cardboard design to a wooden or heavy cardboard block. Print your design on paper or fabric.

JR 10/79

5. Show a greeting card you like and tell how it was printed. Find examples of prints from different countries and times in history or make a scrapbook of different kinds of prints and label each one.

_____

6. Print a wall hanging, picture, decoration on an apron or bandana, or bookplate.

_____

My signature_____

Leader's signature_____ Date badge completed_____

352

Rambler

Purpose: To discover some of the secrets of nature.

When you complete a requirement, have leader initial and date it.

1. Go on walks or hikes with family or friends and make a list of the different places where you find wildlife. Observe two of the following: Insect moving its mouth parts. Creatures that live under rotting logs or loose boards. Garden snail's heart pulsing when it is turned upside down and the bottom of its shell is moistened. Moths or butterflies laying their eggs.

2. Identify four or more migrating birds as they pass through your area in the spring or fall. OR Make up a game that uses pictures of birds.

3. Use a magnifying glass to explore a seashore or edge of a stream, pond, or lake. Write down your discoveries or make a collection of some of the nonliving ones to exhibit.

JR 9/15/79

4. Make a plaster cast of an animal track. OR Develop a short nature trail and label at least ten objects along the way.

JR 9/15/79

5. Tell how to recognize and avoid poisonous plants. Know what to do if you brush against them.

JR 9/15/79

6. Make a terrarium or an arrangement of plants, ferns, mosses, lichens, cactus, and similar things common to your part of the country. OR Make a winter bouquet.

JR. 9/15/79

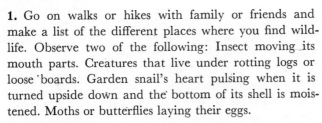

Take a nature walk identify 3 different plants or trees in your area

My signature_____

Leader's signature_____ Date badge completed_____

353

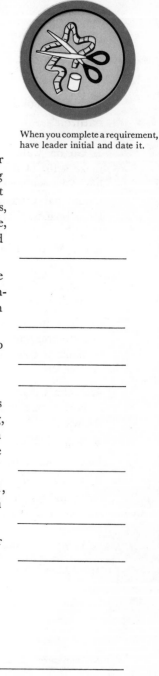

Sewing

Purpose: To start to sew and make something you can use.

When you complete a requirement, have leader initial and date it.

1. Choose two items to make: Tea towel, blouse, four napkins, four place mats, tablecloth, skirt, or something for your meeting place or a camping trip. Then collect equipment for a personal sewing box. Include shears, pins, needles, thread, tape measure, pincushion, thimble, emery bag. Learn sizes and kinds of needles and thread you need and the proper way to use sewing tools.

_____

2. Find different kinds of cotton at home and compare the way each feels. Find out which of these can be laundered and which cannot. Choose cloth that you can wash for things you are making.

_____

3. Name the parts of a sewing machine. Show how to thread it and run it. Practice stitching evenly.

_____

4. Learn how to use pattern books.

_____

5. Do the following: Make plain seams. Finish seams by pinking, overcasting, edge stitching. Show running, hemming, overcasting stitching. Hem, fringe, or bind an edge. Sew on snaps, hooks and eyes, or buttons. Prepare fabric for cutting.

_____

6. Complete the two items you decided on in No. 1, using the skills you have learned. Explain what you did well and what you would like to improve on.

_____

7. List ideas for future sewing you would like to do for yourself, your home and a service project.

_____

My signature_____

Leader's signature_____Date badge completed_____

Skater

Purpose: To learn how to be a good roller skater or ice skater.

1. Tell how to select and care for skates. Explain safety rules for roller skating or ice skating. Show how to stop quickly.

2. Using good form, skate: Forward. Backward. To your left. To your right. Around corners to the left and then to the right.

3. With a partner, skate forward, backward, and in a dance position.

4. Learn to play and teach one skating game.

5. Practice skating to music and be able to do one dance to music.

6. Do a figure eight by tracing a complete circle on one foot, then on the other.

7. Explain or show how to give first aid to a skater who is hurt. Explain how to rescue an ice skater who has fallen through the ice.

8. Read about ice skating or roller skating. Be able to discuss the diet, exercise, and training required for a champion skater. Be able to recognize advanced styles of skating.

9. Help plan and take part in a skating party either indoors or out. OR Make and wear part of a skating costume.

9 — 10 —79

My signature_____

Leader's signature_____Date badge completed_____

355

Songster

Purpose: To learn many songs for different occasions.

1. Sing well with a group the following: Folk song. Art song. Round or canon. Know the source of each song and some interesting information about each.

_____

2. Make a list of songs for opening and closing troop meetings, ceremonies, hiking, and special days at camp. Know how to sing these songs.

_____

3. Sing a program of typical songs of the U.S.A. OR Plan and perform a song program for a national holiday.

_____

4. Tell a legend or folk tale about which a song or other musical composition has been written.

_____

5. Make up actions to go with a song. OR Invent a game using music.

_____

6. Plan and give a program based on the songs and life of a famous composer. OR Plan and give a program on the folk songs of one country, and be able to tell interesting facts about that country's history, customs, and special contribution to the world.

_____

My signature_____

Leader's signature_____Date badge completed_____

Storyteller

Purpose: To read, listen to, and make up stories to tell or read to others.

When you complete a requirement, have leader initial and date it.

1. Read ten different kinds of stories out loud to yourself. Keep a file of stories that you think are good to tell. Make a note on each card of where you found the story, time it takes you to tell it, and the age group that would enjoy it.

_____

2. Watch a good storyteller and her listeners to see what she does to add to the interest of the story. Discuss what makes a storyteller interesting and why people like to listen to a good storyteller.

_____

3. Find or write a story about a place you traveled to. Tell it to your troop or camp group.

_____

4. Find in your dictionary a definition of some words you do not know. Learn to pronounce them and use them correctly.

_____

5. Practice telling several stories from your file to a friend or your patrol. Select the one you do best and tell it to a larger group.

_____

My signature_____

Leader's signature_____ Date badge completed_____

Toymaker

Purpose: To make toys or games for children.

When you complete a requirement, have leader initial and date it.

1. Choose a group of children for whom you want to make toys or games. Find out what kinds of toys children that age would enjoy. Explain which materials are safe to use and why.

J·R 9/14/79

2. Bring to a troop meeting samples of toys and games to help you decide which you want to make.

J R 9/14/79

3. Practice on scrap materials, using tools you will use to make the toys or games.

J R 9/14/79

4. Spend four or more meetings or afternoons helping to make or repair toys or games.

J R 10/30/79

5. Check the toys or games you have made to be sure they are completely finished and any necessary directions have been included.

J R 11/79

6. Help wrap and pack the toys or games to give to the children.

J R 12/79

My signature_____

Leader's signature_____*Joan Reder*___Date badge completed___*12/79*___

358

Troop Camper

Purpose: To learn and practice the things you need to know to go troop camping.

When you complete a requirement, have leader initial and date it.

1. Help your troop plan and carry out a trip to a cabin, cabin unit, or cottage for at least two nights. Help plan where, when, and how to go; what to take and wear; what to do; what permissions are needed. Know something about the site and what is provided there. Help plan the expenses.

_____

2. Help plan suitable meals. Make food lists. Secure, pack, carry, store, prepare, and serve food. Clean up. Plan and cook one meal outside.

_____

3. Use a kaper chart that gives each girl a turn at different camp jobs.

_____

4. Know how to make a bedroll or tie up your sleeping bag. Dress for the expected weather and for the activities you have planned. Have your equipment well tied together.

_____

5. Plan or be responsible for one of the following activities on the weekend: Flag ceremony, outdoor game, nature trail, hike, campfire program, activities for weather that keeps you indoors, grace for a meal, outdoor good turn. Plan equipment needed.

_____

6. Help plan times for getting up in the morning and getting settled at night, times for meals and rest.

_____

7. Help check the troop first aid kit. Talk about emergencies that may occur and what to do about them.

_____

8. Help settle in at the site and, when you leave, help put the site in good condition.

_____

9. After the trip, talk over how the trip went and what you would do differently next time.

_____

My signature_____

Leader's signature_____Date badge completed_____

359

Troop Dramatics

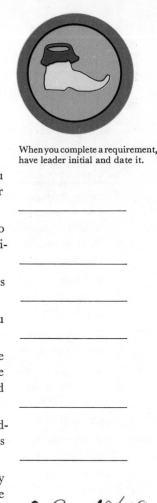

Purpose: To know the first steps in acting and putting on plays.

When you complete a requirement, have leader initial and date it.

1. With your patrol act out three ideas in which you see, hear, taste, feel, or smell. Have your troop discover what you are acting out.

2. Make up a sentence and say it in different ways to show such feelings as: Surprise, alarm, sadness, happiness, fright.

3. Help plan a ceremony for welcoming fly-up Brownies or other new members to your troop.

4. Learn four basic acting terms that will help you on stage.

5. Make up a play about a story from a Girl Guide country. OR Help dramatize an incident from Juliette Low's life. OR Dramatize a historical event or legend connected with your community.

6. Find out what choral reading is. Prepare two readings for a troop ceremony, a campfire, or a parents meeting.

7. Go see a play at a school, church, or community theatre. Discuss what you learned at the performance that would be useful in putting on a troop play. *J R 10/79*

8. With your patrol or others read together two or three plays or stories that could be dramatized. Pick one and decide who will act, make scenery, and make costumes. Present your play to a troop or other group.

My signature_____

Leader's signature_____Date badge completed_____

360

Water Fun

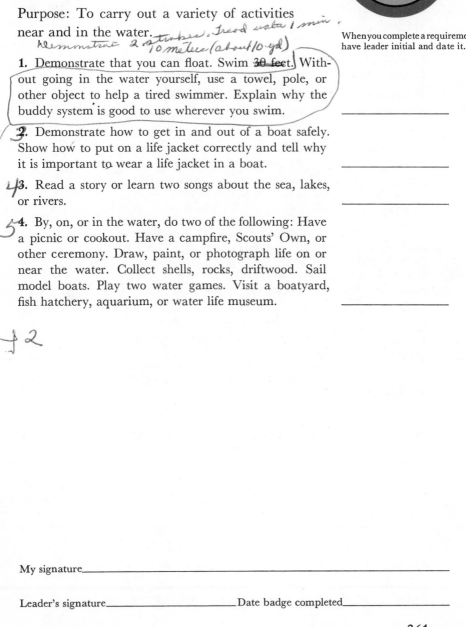

Purpose: To carry out a variety of activities near and in the water. *Demonstrate 2 strokes. Tread water 1 min.*

Demonstrate 2 strokes 10 meters (about 10 yd)

When you complete a requirement, have leader initial and date it.

1. Demonstrate that you can float. Swim ~~30 feet.~~ Without going in the water yourself, use a towel, pole, or other object to help a tired swimmer. Explain why the buddy system is good to use wherever you swim.

_____

2. Demonstrate how to get in and out of a boat safely. Show how to put on a life jacket correctly and tell why it is important to wear a life jacket in a boat.

_____

3. Read a story or learn two songs about the sea, lakes, or rivers.

_____

4. By, on, or in the water, do two of the following: Have a picnic or cookout. Have a campfire, Scouts' Own, or other ceremony. Draw, paint, or photograph life on or near the water. Collect shells, rocks, driftwood. Sail model boats. Play two water games. Visit a boatyard, fish hatchery, aquarium, or water life museum.

_____

My signature_____

Leader's signature_____Date badge completed_____

361

Weaving and Basketry

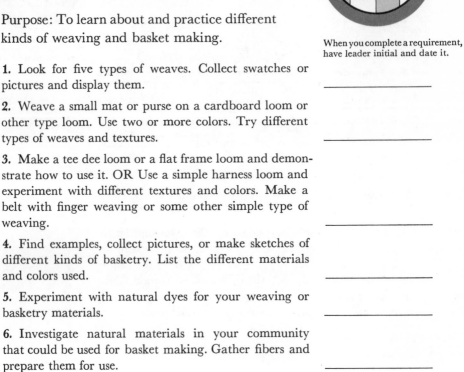

Purpose: To learn about and practice different kinds of weaving and basket making.

When you complete a requirement, have leader initial and date it.

1. Look for five types of weaves. Collect swatches or pictures and display them.

_____

2. Weave a small mat or purse on a cardboard loom or other type loom. Use two or more colors. Try different types of weaves and textures.

_____

3. Make a tee dee loom or a flat frame loom and demonstrate how to use it. OR Use a simple harness loom and experiment with different textures and colors. Make a belt with finger weaving or some other simple type of weaving.

_____

4. Find examples, collect pictures, or make sketches of different kinds of basketry. List the different materials and colors used.

_____

5. Experiment with natural dyes for your weaving or basketry materials.

_____

6. Investigate natural materials in your community that could be used for basket making. Gather fibers and prepare them for use.

_____

7. Make a basket. Use any one of the methods you have learned.

_____

My signature_____

Leader's signature_____Date badge completed_____

World Neighbor

Purpose: To know more about how other children in the world live.

When you complete a requirement, have leader initial and date it.

1. Tell your troop about one book, game, or magazine published by the World Association that tells about Girl Guides and Girl Scouts in other countries.

_____

2. Explain what the World Association of Girl Guides and Girl Scouts is. With your troop learn and sing "The World Song."

_____

3. Make a scrapbook about children in four different parts of the world. Show some things they do that are alike and the things that are different. OR Play four games from different parts of the world. Learn and sing one song from another country.

_____

4. Find out about three organizations that help children in other countries. Tell your troop about the organizations.

_____

5. Take part in a service project for children in another country. Help prepare a skit showing the purpose of the project, why this service is needed, and something about the children who receive the service.

_____

6. Be familiar with the Girl Scout _Say It_ card. Learn to say "hello," "goodbye," "please," and "thank you" in two languages other than English.

_____

7. With your troop or patrol, plan and give a play showing: How you would welcome a girl from another country to your community. What you would show her. How you would talk to her if she did not know English. What you could learn from her.

_____

My signature_____

Leader's signature_____Date badge completed_____

World Games

Purpose: To learn, play, and be able to lead games played around the world.

When you complete a requirement, have leader initial and date it.

1. Choose six Girl Guide/Girl Scout countries and play one game from each country.

2. Discuss safety precautions that need to be taken when playing games with others.

3. Play and be able to lead four of the following kinds of games: Singing game. Action game for children younger than yourself. Get-acquainted game. Circle game. Wide game. Stalking game. Nature game. Relay. Tag game. Quiet game. Paper and pencil game. Testing game.

4. For a play day with your troop or other group, be able to lead and participate in one team ball game or one skill game. OR Help make some troop game equipment.

5. With your patrol plan three games for convalescent or handicapped children.

6. With your troop or patrol plan a world games party and invite another troop or patrol to it. Have an exhibit of books with games from other countries.

My signature_____

Leader's signature_____Date badge completed_____

Writer

Purpose: To try different kinds of writing so
you will know more about being a writer.

When you complete a requirement,
have leader initial and date it.

1. Jot down in a notebook ideas you would like to write
about. Write at least 150 words about one of them.
Share what you have written with your patrol. _____

2. Prepare four issues of a troop newspaper with: News.
Feature stories. Reports of meetings. Notice of future
events. Interviews. _____

3. Correspond with a friend or relative about what you
enjoy most in Girl Scouting. _____

4. Write a poem giving your thoughts or feelings about
something or someone. _____

5. Write a story or short play for your patrol to act out
for your troop or other group. _____

6. Choose a favorite legend or folk tale and write it as
a puppet show or a play. _____

7. Write a report of some of your troop activities for
your council, sponsoring group, or school bulletin. _____

8. Find out how a writer's manuscript is turned into a
printed book. _____

My signature_____

Leader's signature_____ Date badge completed_____

INDEX

370

Director, Program Department	**Dr. Catherine M. Broderick**
Director, Materials Production Division	**Warren Goodrich**
Director, Program Development Division	**Margery Lawrence**
Editor-in-Chief	**Frances W. Poster**
Art Director	**Salvatore A. Carbone**
Production Manager	**Emanuel A. Lopez**

Age-Level Adviser	**Marjorie Kuck**
Writers	**Ann McGovern and Marjorie Kuck**
Editor	**Jane Durborow**
Designer	**Graham Jemmett**
Illustrator	**Dan Dickas**
Technical Illustrator	**Charles R. Hunter**

Material for the *Girl Scout Handbooks* was developed by many people including: Betty Gene Alley □ Marion L. Barrett □ Alethea T. Beckhard □ Shirley M. Carson □ Betty H. Collins □ Marian Davis □ Margarite Hall □ Catherine T. Hammett □ Dagmar Edith McGill □ Goldie McGirt □ Carolyn H. Mitchell □ Corinne M. Murphy Madeline S. Murphy □ Helen M. Quackenbush □ Alice S. Rivoire □ Julian H. Salomon □ Mary M. Weeks □ Carol Weiss □ Marian F. Weller □ Alice White

Girl Scouts of the U.S.A. wishes to thank the hundreds of people across the country who have contributed ideas and critical review for the *Handbooks*. Girls, leaders, members of national committees, national board members and officers, other national staff members, as well as educators and educational departments of commercial organizations have all given graciously of their time, effort, and knowledge. In addition, special consultant help has been given by the following: American Camping Association □ The American Forestry Association □ American Home Economics Association □ The American Humane Association □ American Meteorological Society □ American Museum of Natural History □ American National Red Cross American Society of Mammalogists □ American Veterinary Medical Association American Youth Hostels □ Animal Welfare Institute □ Bicycle Institute of America □ Brookhaven National Laboratory □ Evaporated Milk Association □ Griffith Park Zoo, Los Angeles, California □ The National Audubon Society □ National Aviation Education Council □ National Dairy Council □ National Safety Council □ New York Botanical and Brooklyn Botanic Gardens □ New York Public Library □ New York University □ New York Zoological Society □ The Ninety-Nines □ The Soap and Detergent Association □ state departments of public instruction □ Teachers College, Columbia University □ U.S. National Commission for UNESCO □ U.S. Department of Agriculture □ University of Illinois